ROMAN PERMAN

JESUS,
New Judaism,
Bibleism,
United Religion,

AND LIFE AFTER DEATH,

Also, America and Israel

FROM THE AUTHOR: In this case I do not consider it necessary for someone to represent me, to describe any of my merits. They do not matter. The important thing is the reason this book was written, what questions it answers. Here are the main ones:

Which religion or which groups of related religions are most consistent with the truth? What unites followers of all religions? What is the complete picture of existing and potentially possible religions? **Is there life after death? What options for a future afterlife may be true, and which are a clear delusion?** What is the most convincing evidence of god's existence? Is there eternal punishment? A number of new potential religions are proposed. **A new religion, Karmaism,** is proposed and substantiated, and on its basis - **the United Religion that unites all humanistic religions, as well as the Punishism religion, which speak of the inevitable punishment for violations of moral norms.** An explanation is given for what is considered bad behavior, not only in life, but also in **politics,** using the examples of the situations in America and Israel. **A United Philosophy** is also proposed. **A complete table of all existing and potentially possible humanistic religions is provided.** It is shown which of them can most likely correspond to the truth, and which practically have no serious grounds for this. Based on the analysis of the Gospels, **a solution to the mission of Jesus Christ is proposed and a rationale is given for the new unifying religions of New Judaism, Common Judaism, Bibleism, Newarism and Prophetism;** including those religions which consider it necessary to fulfill the covenants of God set forth in the Torah that apply to all people, and not only to the Jews: this is also **Bibleism, Newarism, New Judaism and Prophetism, and also Injudaism. The author analyzes the grounds for belief in life after death from the point of view of the available facts and existing religious ideas on this topic.** The ones selected are those which **have the greatest chances to correspond with the truth.**

CONTENTS

Jesus..1

Injudaism 42

Judaism, Profetism, Invoism, Messian Christianity...........................49

Unifying Religions 53

Bibleism 55

Newarism..61

New Judaism 63

Uphism 72

Karmaism 75

United Religion (Uarism) And Punishism 84

The United States Of America 91

Israel...99

Life After Death 110

Table Of Existing And Potentially Possible Religions.......................121

JESUS

Religion still plays a very large role in our world. And there are not so few religions. Each of them claims that only it is right, that only it owns the truth. I would like to understand which of them are clearly false, and which have a chance **to correspond to the truth.** Whatever I may personally believe, I believe that this is extremely important for the fate of the world. After all, religions do not exist by themselves, they largely determine the mentality of this or that nation and its attitude towards other nations. I would like faith not to be blind, to be chosen not only by feelings or by belonging to a particular nation, but also by reason, rejecting what common sense rebels against, i.e., clearly false religions.

First of all, I appeal to those who believe in the One God - the Creator. The overwhelming majority of believers belong to them. In history, not so many manifestations of God are known to people. And all these were appearances to individual people – to the prophets, through whom He transmitted information to the people of the Earth. These were individual meetings, without witnesses, "vision meetings," there was no one to certify them. The manifestation of God at once **to many people,** to the entire Jewish people, which took place at Mount Sinai during the wanderings of the Jews in the Sinai desert after leaving Egypt, **is the only and completely unique case in history.** Of course, no one saw the Almighty with their own eyes, it is possible that this is completely impossible. But the clear signs of His appearance, about which He warned the people in advance through Moses (Moshe) - smoke, fire, trembling of the mountain, thunder, and lightning - were seen by everyone. This is how it is described in the Torah:

"And God said, addressing Moshe: 'Here I am coming to you in a thick cloud, so that the people will hear <u>how I will speak with you</u>, and they will also believe in you forever ... Go to the people and sanctify it today and tomorrow, let them wash their clothes to be ready for the third day, for on the third day God will descend in front of all the people on Mount Sinai.'

'And it was - on the third day, when morning came, thunder thundered, and lightning flashed, and a thick cloud hid the mountain, and the shofar sounded very loudly, and all the people who were in the camp shuddered, and Moses led the people out of the camp to meet the Almighty and stood at the foot of the mountain.'

And Mount Sinai was all smoking because God descended on it in fire, and the smoke from it ascended like smoke from a furnace, and the whole mountain shook violently ... And the All-Mighty spoke all these words, saying:

'I am God, your Almighty, who brought you out of the land of Egypt, out of the house of slavery. May you have no other gods besides Me.

Do not make yourself a statue and any image ... Do not worship them and do not serve them ...

Do not say the name of God, your Almighty, in vain ...

Remember the sabbath day to keep it holy. Work six days and do all your work, and the seventh day, Saturday, to God your Almighty: do not do any work, neither you, nor your son, nor your daughter, nor your servant, nor your cattle ... In six days God created heaven and earth, the sea and all that is in them, and rested on the seventh day; therefore God blessed and sanctified the sabbath day.

Honor your father and your mother, so that your days on the Earth, which God, your Almighty, gives you, may be prolonged.

Do not kill.

Do not commit adultery.

Do not steal.

Do not speak false testimony of your neighbor.

Do not covet your neighbor's house; do not covet your neighbor's wife, nor his servant, nor his bull, nor his donkey, and nothing that is with your neighbor."

And all the people saw sounds, and flames, and the sound of the shofar, and a steaming mountain; and when the people saw, they shuddered and stood at a distance. And they said to Moshe: "Speak with us, and we will hear, let the Almighty not speak to us, otherwise we will die" (Torah, Book of Shemot 20, chapter Yitro).

And even before that there was a chain of astonishing and amazing events witnessed and participated by the Jewish people - the so-called "Egyptian executions" - a terrible drought, flood, locust infestation, etc., for 10 years in a row - and how the Jews miraculously managed to escape from the Pharaoh's troops (the waters of the Red Sea gulf parted and allowed them to pass, and then closed up and absorbed the pharaoh's vanguard). Whether this happened for sure or not, the fact is that the salvation of the Jews in such a situation was a real miracle.

We do not know what the nature of God is, there may be a variety of opinions on this topic, but there is no other fact similar in persuasiveness, showing that at least the Ten Commandments may have been transmitted to us by God Himself. And if you do not believe this, then all the more so you cannot believe all the other prophets. Therefore, for those who believe in God, **the true religion should be based on the Ten Commandments given by God and on being their continuation the Torah and the Bible.**

About Jesus, who is the main reason for the discrepancy between Judaism and Christianity. As you know, Jesus Christ was a Jew (in his earthly life) - he was born a Jew and grew up among the Jews. Jesus is the Greek interpretation of his name, in Hebrew it sounded Yeshua or Yeshu, which is an abbreviation of his full name Yehoshua, and Christ means an Envoy or mediator, in this case, the Envoy of God. Naturally, he was raised in Judaism. And he recognized himself as a Jew. Not once in his passionate sermons did he express opinions that seriously contradict Judaism. And this is natural. After all, God gave the Jewish people the Ten Commandments and the Torah - the basis of the Jewish religion; every Jew knew it. And Jesus did not question them in the least. In fact, he **preached Judaism**. Moreover, he fought against violations of the requirements of Judaism. Jesus said (see the Gospel of Matthew 5: 17-18, - the second most written and most informative of the Gospels): **"Do not think that I have come to break the law (Torah) or the prophets ... Truly I say to you, until heaven and earth pass away, not a single thing will pass from the law."** "So, whoever breaks one of these commandments ... he will be called the least one in the Kingdom of Heaven; and whoever does and teaches, he will be called great in the Kingdom of Heaven" (ibid., 5:19). "Not everyone who says to Me: "Lord! God!" will enter the kingdom of heaven, but he who does the will of my Father in heaven" (7:21). The Gospel of Luke: "But rather heaven and earth will pass away than one line of the law will be lost" ((16:17). "Do not commit adultery; do not kill; do not steal; do not bear false witness; honor your father and your mother" (18:22). As you can see, Jesus insists on the full fulfillment of the laws given by the Almighty, which is the essence of traditional Judaism. The first Gospel was written by Mark

(John-Mark). It was written 10-15 years after the execution of Jesus Christ, mainly according to the stories of Peter, who was the closest companion of Jesus and after his execution became the head of the first Judeo-Christian community. I call it that because in the first decades of its existence there was still no clear division into Jewish and Christian religions, and those who recognized Jesus did not at all think that they had switched to another religion, having abandoned the faith of the fathers. They observed all the requirements of traditional Judaism, differing from those around them only by the preaching that the Messiah had already come, was already with them, as well as a particularly strong preaching of mercy, which was the main content of what Jesus taught. The Gospel of Mark was created shortly after the execution of Jesus and, obviously, had not yet had time to acquire many myths that arose later, i.e., it is the most trustworthy. Here are the important commandments of Jesus cited in it: "The first commandment: 'Hear, Israel! The Lord our God is One Lord; And you shall love the Lord your God with all your heart, and with all your soul, and with all your mind, and with all your strength.' Behold, the first commandment! The second is similar to it: "Love your neighbor as yourself;" there is no other greater commandment than these" (12: 29-31); "Whoever wants to be the first, be the last of all and a servant to all" (9:35); "How difficult it is for those who hope for riches to enter the Kingdom of God! It is easier for a camel to pass through the ears of a needle than for a rich man to enter the Kingdom of God" (10: 24,25); On the possibility of certain activities on Saturday: "**Saturday for man, not man for Saturday**" (2:27), - Jesus' only "correction" to the Ten Commandments and, in general, to the commandments of the Torah. The only serious "heresy" of Jesus was that he said that he was already in the Kingdom of Heaven and made it clear that he is the Envoy of God. He did not preach any other judgments that could give rise to another religion. Everything he said fit into mainstream Judaism. The split of Judaism and the emergence of Christianity from a part of it

5

occurred in connection with the execution of Jesus, with the decision of the question of whether he was the Messiah. At the first stage, the main contradictions between the Christian and Jewish religions were questions about whether Jesus was the Messiah - the Savior and what commandments of the Most High Christians should fulfill. These contradictions did not prevent them from coexisting within the same religion. At the present time, after the adoption of the doctrine of the Trinity, **the main contradiction between Christianity and Judaism is the question of whether Jesus is God. There are also serious questions about whether Jesus is the Messiah, I mean, the future Messiah, as well as whether he was the Envoy of God from God's Kingdom, or just a prophet, i.e., a person through whom God transmitted information to people, or whether he acted on his own behalf, having no connection with God.** Less important are questions about the priority between works and one's faith and the need for baptism. The rest are not fundamental.

About Jesus as the Messiah. Who is a Messiah? Judging by the sacred books of the Old Testament, a Messiah is a mediator between God and people who should bring peace and prosperity to Earth. This must be a very powerful person, a "king" who will establish peace and just order and be able to force the peoples opposing him to submit to his will. This is what the Prophets say: "He will rule from sea to sea and from the river to the ends of the earth" (Psalms 72: 8). "And they will hammer their swords into plowshares, and their spears into sickles; the people will not lift up the sword against nation, and they will learn war no more" (Isaiah 2: 4). "And with the rod of his mouth he will smite the earth" (Isaiah 11: 4 - about the Messiah). Jesus had nothing of the kind. He was not a "king" and did not bring peace and prosperity to the Earth. He could not fulfill even the very minimum that could only be expected from the Messiah (and which was really expected by all Jews) - to make life easier, at least for the Jewish people, to which, in his own words, he was sent, to liberate the Jewish state from Roman rule. On the contrary, after his arrival, terrible misfortunes befell the Jews. That is, it is quite clear that Jesus did not meet the prediction of the Messiah. Then the following explanation appeared, which is common to almost all directions of Christianity: Jesus is the Messiah, but this was only his first coming, and his role was to save people from God's punishment hanging over them for the sin of their first parents, Adam and Eve, who disobeyed God and tasted the forbidden fruit. For this they were expelled from paradise and doomed to a hard life. And not only they, but all their descendants. What exactly was this punishment? Here it is: "Cursed is the earth for you ... thorns and thistles will grow for you ... in the sweat of your brow you will eat bread ... for dust you and to dust you will return" (Genesis 3: 16-19). And to the woman: "In hardships you will bear children" (ibid.). Jesus took upon himself the sins of people, which opened the possibility for them not to go to hell - however, only to those who were baptized. Those who did not pass such a ceremony, after death, will be sent to hell, to torment - even those who led the life of a righteous man. According to most directions of Christian teaching, people who have not undergone the rite of baptism bear the guilt for the sin of Adam and Eve and therefore have no chance of salvation, even being righteous. This concept is clearly manifested, for example, in Dante's Divine Comedy, which depicts how the righteous of antiquity are tormented in hell (albeit in its "first circle," the easiest one), because they lived before Jesus and, therefore, could not to be cleansed by baptism from original sin. Judaism teaches that every person receives a pure soul from birth, and it depends only on his own choice, on his behavior - to make it sinful or righteous and pure. A person should not be punished for the sins of his ancestors, let alone our most ancient ancestors. Everyone will answer before God only for their own sins. I am convinced that this is exactly the case: I cannot imagine that God the Creator, for whom we are all His creations, His children, is so unfair as to punish the innocent, or punish a person for his philosophical and religious views, and not for his behavior, his specific actions. By the way, according to the predictions of the prophets, the Messiah must be from the family of King David. In the Gospel of Mark, not a word is said about Jesus' descent from King David. He could not have been unaware of this prediction and would certainly have written about it if it had been true. The Gospel of Matthew begins with tracing the lineage of Jesus, who allegedly descends from King David. But Jesus never said that he was a descendant of King David (which should be the foretold Messiah). If this were so, I think Jesus himself would not have kept silent about this, and such an important fact, one of the proofs that Jesus is the Messiah, would have entered the first Gospel of Mark. However, this did not happen. In response to a direct question about this, Jesus says that he cannot be a descendant of King David, because he lived even before him, and King David called him Lord: "So if David calls Him (Christ) Lord, how is He his son?" (22: 41-45). But it is clear that we are talking about that Jesus Christ who lives the life of an earthly man - this earthly Jesus, if he is the Messiah, must be, according to the prophets, be a descendant of King David. In addition, his lineage is traced back to Joseph: "Jacob gave birth to Joseph, the husband of Mary, from whom Jesus was born, called Christ." But if the conception was "immaculate," and Joseph is not the biological father of Jesus, then Jesus is not a direct descendant of King David. At best, he could be his maternal descendant, but this is not clearly stated or traced.

As we all know, the coming of Jesus did not change anything in the first part of the "punishment given by God," nor in the second. We still earn our bread in the sweat of our brow, and women give birth in agony. It is logical to assume that the third part of it, about baptism, introduced by Christianity, does not correspond to reality. It is absolutely impossible to believe that good people, by the will of their Creator, should suffer without any guilt or only for their convictions, and some villain can "forgive" his sins and will be rewarded with paradise just because he was baptized. This is completely inconsistent with the ideas of the Judaists and my personal idea of a God who loves His creatures. In addition, if this or that person did not believe in God or doubted His existence, then this is hardly decisive after his death, when he had already appeared before God and was convinced that He exists. But the deeds of a person speak about his soul, about his guilt or innocence, about his wonderful spiritual qualities or about his baseness, about whether he fulfilled the covenants of God. And this, of course, is very important, it should be decisive for the Lord's decision on the future fate of the human soul. The presence of many beautiful, selfless people, including among unbelievers, proves the inconsistency of the myth of the original depravity, sinfulness of every person, which can only be redeemed by the rite of baptism and prayers. If we understand well the difference between the main merits of a person and the small flaws that each of us encounters, and can understand whether he is a good person or not, then really the Great Creator Himself cannot understand this? No, it's impossible to believe. Therefore, I am sure: **the main result of God's judgment depends on the deeds of a person, and no rituals and prayers can be saved from His justice, and everyone will receive what he deserves with his actions, his deeds, his life.** This is one of the cornerstones of Judaism. This does not mean at all that it is impossible to "forgive" sins at all - a person, obviously, can be forgiven, but only in the case of sincere repentance, confirmed by his deeds.

But what about Jesus then? He was undoubtedly an outstanding personality. His fantastic abilities, his passionate speeches in defense of the observance of God's covenants, his tremendous power of preaching mercy, humility, meekness, love, his steadfastness, and martyrdom cannot but impress. Perhaps he really was a prophet, one of the prophets of

Judaism, through whom God conveyed important information to people. Unfortunately, we cannot know this for sure, Jesus could have been just an impostor, of which there were quite a few then, and maybe even the Envoy of the Most High, His Son - although this option is very doubtful. However, it is also obvious that he was not the Messiah, since he did not accomplish anything that the Messiah was supposed to do - that is a fact. I am convinced that the life and painful death of Jesus is not a "puncture," not a failure of the Lord. It was just that **Jesus was not destined to become the Messiah; he had a different mission.** After all, to be Christ, i.e., the Envoy of God or the prophet - the mediator between Him and people, does not mean to be the Messiah, i.e., to those who must bring peace and prosperity to Earth. You can't hold an equal sign here. After all, Jesus, if he was a prophet, was not the only prophet of God on Earth, and each of them had their own tasks.

Now, on the teachings of Jesus, the essence of his sermons. Here are the main points of Jesus' teaching, broken it down into three parts. The first part is not objectionable and lies entirely in the mainstream of Judaism. The second and third are very problematic. So, here are the direct statements of Jesus, cited in the Gospels of Matthew and Luke (links without letters, only numbers for chapters and verses (paragraphs).

First part. About mercy, meekness, the need to fulfill God›s commandments.

The Gospel of Matthew: "Blessed are the meek, for they will inherit the earth. Blessed are those who hunger and thirst for righteousness, for they will be satisfied. Blessed are the merciful, for they will have mercy. Blessed are the pure in heart, for they will see God. Blessed are the peacemakers, for they will be called sons of God. Blessed are those cast out for righteousness, for theirs is the kingdom of heaven" (5: 5-10). "Everyone who is angry with his brother in vain is subject to judgment" (5:22). "Give to him who asks of you, and don't turn away from him who wants to borrow from you" (5:42). "Do not do your charity in front of people so that they may see you: otherwise, you will not have a reward from your Father in Heaven" (6: 1). "If you forgive people their sins, then your Heavenly Father will forgive you too; And if you will not forgive people their sins, then your Father will not forgive you your sins" (6: 14,15). "Judge not lest ye be judged; For with what judgment you judge, you will be judged; and with what measure you mete, it will be measured to you also. And why are you looking at the mote in your brother's eye, but you don't feel the beam in your eye? " (7: 1-3). "So, in everything you want people to do to you, so do you to them; for in this is the law and the prophets" (7:12). "See that you despise not one of these little ones" (8:10). "Then Peter came to him and said: Lord! How many times should I forgive my brother who sins against me? Up to seven times? Jesus says to him: I do not say to you: "up to seven," but up to seventy times seventy" (8: 21,22). "Whoever wants to be great among you, let him be your servant; And whoever wants to be the first among you, let him be your slave" (20: 26,27). The Gospel of Luke: "If you do not repent, you will all perish in the same way" (13: 3). "He who exalts himself will be humbled, but he who humbles himself will be exalted" (14:11). "Call the poor and the crippled to the feast" (14:13). "If your brother sins against you, reprimand him, and if he repents, forgive him; And if he sins against you seven times a day and turns back seven times a day and says I repent, forgive him" (17: 3,4).

The second part is about the benefits of suffering and poverty on Earth.

The Gospel of Matthew: "Blessed are they that mourn, for they will be comforted" (5: 4). "Do not lay up for yourselves treasures on the earth, where moth and rust destroy, and where thieves break in and steal; But lay up for yourselves treasures in heaven ... For where your treasure is, there your heart will also be" (6: 19-21). "But he who endures to the end will be saved" (24: 3). The Gospel of Luke: "Sell your estates and give alms" (12:33). "All that you have, sell and give to the poor, and you will have treasure in heaven" (18:22). "A certain man was rich ... and feasted every day. There was also a beggar named Lazarus, who was lying at his gate in scabs ... The beggar died and was carried by the angels into Abraham's bosom; the rich man also died and was buried; and in hell, being in torment, he lifted his eyes, saw Abraham and Lazarus in the distance against his background, and cried out, said: Father Abraham! Have mercy on me and send Lazarus to dip the end of his finger in water and cool my tongue, for I am tormented in this flame. But Abraham said: child! Remember that you have already received your good in your life, and Lazarus has received evil; now he is comforted here, and you are suffering; And besides all this, a great gulf is established between us and you, so that those who want to pass from here to you cannot, nor do they pass from there to us" (16: 19-26).

Concerning the requirement to completely distribute wealth, in my opinion, this is certainly an unjustified exaggeration. Without a monetary incentive, society could not exist. But all measures must be taken, everything that is possible, to reduce the huge gap between the richest and the poorest, the existence of which is unfair and disproportionate: it does not correspond to the abilities and merits or demerits of the absolutely poor and overly rich people. And in general, the thesis that in this life there is no need to strive for happiness, that you need to think exclusively about life after death, that happiness in this life turns into suffering in the future life, raises great doubts and protest. I think that the result of God's judgment does not depend on whether a person was rich or not, but on how he behaved in life, whether he achieved wealth in an honest way, whether he shared with the poor, etc.; from what this person is, what his soul is like. The same, as life shows, is the attitude of the overwhelming number of people to this situation, including believers and Christian clergy. Striving for happiness in this life is natural and does not violate God's commandments - just do not behave meanly, do not deceive, win honestly, think not only of yourself, but also of others.

The third part is about non-resistance to evil (at least by violence).

The Gospel of Matthew (Luke does not say this explicitly): "Do not resist the evil one. But whoever slaps you on your right cheek, turn the other to him also; And whoever wants to sue you and take your shirt, give him your outer garment; And whoever forces you to go one mile with him, go with him two ... Love your enemies, bless those who curse you, do good to those who hate you, and pray for those who offend you and persecute you ... reward? Do not the tax collectors do the same? And if you greet only your brothers, what are you doing special? Do not the Gentiles do the same?" (5: 39-41,44-47).

This theory, like most other ideas, is only good to a certain extent and, if taken to an extreme, goes from good to evil. After all, if evil is not resisted, then it will win everything that is possible from good and destroy or turn into slaves its carriers. Therefore, without denying the need for love or, at least, understanding and condescension, it should be recognized that non-resistance to evil is possible and necessary only until it becomes clear that in this particular case, good is not appreciated, but only encourages evil and leads, thus, to even greater evil. There is an area in which this theory does not apply at all - these are cases when it comes to communicating with people or groups of people who are fanatics of a false idea, aggressive towards other groups, and therefore unable to appreciate the good, considering it only a manifestation of weakness. This was Nazism, which welcomed the violation of God's main commandment - "Thou shalt not kill," do not take away from a person his most important asset - life itself. In such cases, non-resistance to evil, including violence, threatens terrible disasters and is tantamount to crime. It is not without reason that the wisdom of Judaism reads: "Eradicate evil from your midst" (Torah, Book of Deut. 21:21, 24: 7), "The merciful to the cruel is cruel to the merciful" (Kohelet Rabbah 7:13). Yes, and Jesus himself retreated from his call: "I did not come to bring peace, but a sword" (against those who would deny me - Matthew 10:34).

Another thing is that you need to be tolerant, not to succumb to anger, not to be too proud, to be able to understand and forgive, not to rush to fight back, responding to evil with evil, and to give the person who offended you the opportunity to calmly understand the situation. You need to be able to politely but firmly explain to him your point of view and the incorrectness of his behavior. If this is a good person, then sooner or later he will understand, and he will be ashamed. This interpretation completely coincides with what Judaism teaches, according to which anger is a grave sin.

It is possible that Jesus deliberately exaggerated, clothed the ideas of suffering and non-resistance to evil in such an extreme, paradoxical form, knowing that it is hardly possible to fully implement them in real life, but presenting these ideas in such an extreme form will greatly enhance the desire to observe them. This especially concerns the need not to conceal evil and think a hundred times and use all other ways before responding with an insult to an insult, evil for evil.

It is clear that Jesus Christ has statements that hardly correspond to the truth and do not allow the majority of Judaists to recognize him as a prophet. He said that he was a companion of God and after death he will return to Earth, and soon, so that his contemporaries will see it (which did not happen): "Then they will see the Son of Man coming in the clouds with great power and glory. And then He will send His angels and gather His elect from the four winds, from the end of the earth to the end of heaven ... Truly I say to you: this generation will not pass away, as all this will be" (Mark 13: 26-30). The prophet could not but recognize the need to wash his hands before eating and claim eternal torment in hell with such a short earthly life. But unfortunately, he did not leave any notes. Most likely, **he was slandered** by his disciples in the heat of competition with other currents of Judaism. The non-recognition by Judaism that Jesus is, perhaps, a prophet gives rise to the misconceptions that Judaism is further from Christianity, and even from the Messianic Christianity created by the Jews, than Islam, which is actually very far from it, but recognizes Jesus as one of the prophets. US President Adams wrote: "The Jews were chosen to store and transmit to all mankind the idea of a Supreme Mind, mighty and wise, which is the great foundation of all morality, of all civilization. They are the most beautiful nation ever to inhabit this earth. They gave religion to three quarters of humanity." But the mission is not complete. We must try to correct what has been misinterpreted and unite the majority on the basis of truth.

I want to emphasize once again that Jesus did not leave any records, and we can judge about him only by the texts of the Gospels, which inevitably include not only the truth, but also myths that arose later. This is especially true of the Gospels, written much later than the events described in them, i.e., the Gospels of Matthew, Luke, and even more so of John. Naturally, by the time they were written, new legends and myths about the coming of Jesus had appeared, and some of them, as you can see, became part of these Gospels. Something has been changed, something new has been introduced. Any rumor, any news over time is usually overgrown with various changes and additions. This law cannot fail to apply in the event of dissemination of information about the activities and execution of Jesus. The content of what has been written cannot but be influenced, to one degree or another, by the "political situation," which clearly affected the Gospel of John. And the previous Gospels were written in conditions of opposition of the new religious trend to the existing traditional trends, in the conditions of the struggle for the minds of people. Therefore, the degree of trust in these Gospels and, moreover, in the Gospel of John, created much later, cannot be absolute and even the same as in the Gospel of Mark, although everything said to a certain extent applies to the latter. Here is what the writer Vladimir Tendryakov writes in his story *Attempt on Mirages*: "The stratification began immediately after the tragic death of Jesus. There were not only stories about him, but also tall tales. His biographies appeared later. In the earliest of the canonical Gospels, from Mark, real features are clearly visible through the legend. Subsequent Evangelists even speculated that the poor preacher turned out to be a descendant of the king - King David. He, of course, did not feed thousands of hungry people with five loaves of bread, he didn't walk on water, as if on dry land, but he probably could restore the ability to move his paralyzed hand, as well as relieve seizures and cleanse nervous eczema." Thus, many things were probably invented, even in the first Gospel of Mark.

Imagine that after the coming of Jesus, only the Gospels would be created and nothing else. Then Christianity in its modern form could hardly have arisen, it would represent one of the directions of Judaism, which differs from others only in the preaching that Jesus was the Messiah, and the strengthening of the idea of mercy given by Jesus to its most extreme manifestations (non-resistance to evil by violence) as well as a reduction in Sabbath requirements and a validation of the concept of an afterlife awaiting us. Most of the requirements of the Torah were removed. Christianity has turned into another religion, which in many ways is an undoubted perversion of what Jesus taught, and directly contradicts his teachings. After all, the removal of most of the requirements of the Torah made it possible to widely spread this religion among non-Jews. Perhaps this was God's intention. But the second Christian "revolution," three hundred years later completed the process, elevating Jesus to the rank of God Himself, His constituent part, God the Son, introducing the mythical Trinity, which no one can clearly explain or understand.

Some passages from the Gospels suggest that their authors, oddly enough, knew little about life in Judea at that time. For example, it is described that, having come to Jerusalem on the eve of Easter, Jesus saw money changers and pens with animals in the courtyard of the temple. "And he found that in the temple they were selling oxen, sheep and doves, and the money changers were sitting. And making a whip of cords, he drove everyone out of the temple, also the sheep and the oxen, and scattered the money of the money changers, and overturned their tables" (John 2:14, 15). But their presence in the courtyard of the Temple, as Solomon Dinkevich writes, for example, in the book *Jews, Judaism, Israel*, "was not only natural, but also necessary for the administration of the temple service. After all, people had to fulfill the command of the Lord: "And let them not appear before God empty-handed, let each bring as much as he can" (Torah, Deut 16: 16,17). For many pilgrims, the road to the Temple took 5-10 days. During this time, it was impossible to keep the sacrificial animals and the first fruits of the harvest in good condition. Therefore, the animals and fruits intended for sacrifice were sold by the Jews at the place of residence and went to the Temple with money. When they came to the Temple, they bought the appropriate animals and fruits. That is why there were money changers and sacrificial animals **in the courtyard of the Temple**. Jesus was a Jew who knew the Law and customs well ... Therefore, he could not in any way be outraged by the centuries-old presence in the courtyard of the Temple, and the sellers of sacrificial animals. What is said in the Gospels raises great doubts.

I would go even further. This example not only raises doubts, but it also undermines the credibility of the texts of the Gospels and their authors, at least in the Gospel of John. If such inventions can be allowed in a question that is not caused by any interest of the authors (since the description of Jesus' behavior in the temple could hardly affect the struggle with other areas of Judaism for influence), then one can imagine what kind of fraud, exaggerations, etc. could be when describing those moments that could play a significant role in the struggle with other religious movements of Judaism for influence on human souls. Obviously, as a consequence of such a struggle, especially a lot of unfounded criticism is contained in the Gospels in relation to the most numerous group of representatives of the Jewish religion of that time - the Pharisees (as a result, the definition of "Pharisees" eventually became synonymous with the definition of "hypocrite"), who believed in the afterlife, and also to those whom Jesus calls scribes, i.e., the people who were experts in the Torah and other books of the Old Testament and who could therefore serve as opponents of any distortion of the Holy Scriptures. Moreover, this criticism is not specific to one or another, but general, aimed at all at once. Jesus calls them "hypocrites," "vipers and the offspring of vipers," and according to the Gospel of John, even "devils and servants of the devil." Although Jesus himself was precisely a Pharisee and spoke constantly about the afterlife, about God's Kingdom, about heaven and hell, the followers of another major direction of Judaism of that time, the Sadducees, generally denied the afterlife. Where did Jesus, who preached mercy, meekness, forgiveness, love, get so much anger towards these people? Did the majority of them not fulfill God's commandments properly and were distinguished by posturing and hypocrisy? But with the level of devotion to faith, the fulfillment of God's commandments, which was at that time, this simply could not be. History shows that almost every one of them was ready to die rather than go to the

18

violation of the Law. Here is an example described in the book of B.V. Pilate (chapter 18):

"Pilate once ordered that the images of the emperor be brought to Jerusalem ... The Jews were in a terrible agitation; those who were near this spectacle were horrified, seeing in it a violation of the Law (since the Jews are prohibited from displaying images in the city) ... Everyone moved to Pilate to ask him to remove the images from Jerusalem and to leave the inviolable faith of their fathers. Having received a refusal from him, they threw themselves on the ground and remained in this position for five days and the same number of nights, without moving. On the sixth day, Pilate sat down in a judge's chair in a large stadium and ordered the people to be called to him in order to announce his decision to them; first, he gave the order to the soldiers: at the given signal, surround the Jews with weapons in their hands. Seeing themselves suddenly enclosed by a triple line of armed soldiers, the Jews were dumbfounded. But when Pilate announced that he would order them all to be hacked if they did not accept the imperial images, and immediately signaled to the soldiers to draw their swords, then the Jews, as if by agreement, all fell to the ground, stretched out their necks and loudly exclaimed: they would rather let themselves be killed, than break the Law. Struck by this religious feat, Pilate gave the order to immediately remove the statues from Jerusalem."

We can only regret once again that Jesus did not leave records, and we must get acquainted with the story of his life and death and with his teaching in the presentation of other people interested in the victory of this teaching.

Many misconceptions of Christianity also arose due to an incorrect translation from Hebrew, - after all, representatives of many peoples who did not speak Hebrew (the Hebrew language now revived in Israel), in which the books of the Old Testament were written, began to be engaged in the development of Christianity. For example, the myth of the Immaculate Conception was born, when the word "alma," which means not "virgin" ("Betula"), but "young, young woman," was translated from Hebrew as "virgin," i.e., virgin, innocent girl. (By the way, this suggests whether, in principle, the Envoy is possible, as we understand him, i.e., the introduction into humanity of the one who was previously with God in God's Kingdom, - after all, the concept of Christ means both the Envoy and the **mediator**)? There are many similar facts. This is especially true for a number of statements interpreted as predictions about the coming of Jesus Christ. The same applies to statements that deliberately present Judaism as a teaching calling for revenge on the offenders, while its most important provisions read: "Without mercy, the world could not stand" (Midrash Bereishit Rabbah), "Be always among the persecuted, not persecutors, among the offended, and not offending" (Talmud, treatise Gittin 36). The Jews, who knew the primary sources well and considered the new religious trend to be a profanation of the Holy Doctrine, were a living denunciation of Christianity. This is one of the reasons why Christians over the centuries have tried to convert them to "the faith of Christ" or to destroy them. By the way, those rare Christians - experts in Hebrew who tried to pay attention to the substitutions in Christianity - were also persecuted - they were forced to remain silent. In the end, the "creative development" of Christianity led to the fact that **Jesus was made God Himself,** and the Old Testament was practically forgotten - they began to say that **Jesus allegedly introduced a new law (New Testament), which changes the conditions of the previous Covenant given by God people of the Earth** and leads to a new teaching - Christianity. Christianity began to be called the "New Israel," i.e., "True," "modern" Israel, called upon to replace the Jewish people in dialogue with God. **It turned out that Judaism is nothing, it is supposedly abolished, and its bearers are Jews, criminals who "killed God."** Hostility and hatred towards Jews developed everywhere and was specially implanted by the Church, anti-Semitism intensified.

I think to understand what the mission of Jesus Christ really was, you need to discard all judgments that are not supported by real life and see what has changed in the world in connection with his coming, fulfilling the covenant given by the Bible: "Judge them by their fruits." And then we will see that the only real change, the impetus for which was the life and martyrdom of Jesus, is only one: **a new religious trend of extraordinary missionary power** arose in Judaism, which, having transformed over time into a new, Christian, religion, was able to ensure the widest spread to the land of monotheism, - faith in the One God. I think the answer to the life and death of Jesus is this:

If Jesus really is a prophet through whom God conveyed important information to people, including the very fact of his execution and subsequent resurrection, then **his mission was to ensure the victory of monotheism on Earth - faith in the One God and the need to fulfill His Commandments**. By doing so, he completed what Abraham and Moses had begun. His extraordinary sermons and his execution made a huge impression on people and turned out to be a powerful stimulant, which eventually gave rise to a new religious movement, which managed to eliminate all obstacles to the wide dissemination of the Basic Law among the peoples of the Earth, expressed long before that by His Lord His Ten Commandments (which became the basis as Jewish, and, almost completely, of this new, Christian, religion), and ultimately - to ensure the victory of monotheism over paganism. One can understand how important this is for the Creator. And **only in this way could the ground be prepared for the coming of the Messiah**.

What was needed for this? A fascinating teaching to people that they will surely have an afterlife, and in the case of good behavior, eternal bliss in

21

paradise, a decrease in unnecessarily harsh requirements for the Sabbath, an increase in humanistic requirements and an impressive execution of the preacher. All this was done. The first was of particular importance. After all, the conclusion about the afterlife does not directly follow from the Torah. Therefore, at that time, the two leading branches of Judaism looked at this issue differently. The Pharisees believed in an afterlife, but the Sadducees did not. And the requirements for the Sabbath were apparently deemed too harsh and hindered the widespread adoption of monotheism. I think that, most likely, the resulting new religious direction should have been **one of the directions of Judaism, differing from it only by confirming the correctness of faith in the afterlife, reducing the level of requirements for the Sabbath, strengthening the humanistic component and its missionary orientation**. And in the first period after the emergence of Christianity, so it actually was. But, as you know, in fact, this later led to the creation of a new religion. And this new, Christian religion perfectly coped with the rapid spread of monotheism across the Earth - faith in the One God. However, unfortunately, over time, it has gone too far from its "origins," from what Jesus himself and the first Christians, including his immediate disciples, preached. After all, a significant part of what forms the basis of today's Christian teaching was written later and, in many ways, contradicts what they taught.

In my opinion, in order to correctly judge the essence of Jesus' mission, it is necessary to abstract from all secondary issues, statements, which for the most part could have been conveyed by the authors of the Gospels and his disciples incorrectly (and that does not allow us to recognize the possibility that he could be a prophet of God), and **focus only on the most important thing, i.e., on teaching about God's Kingdom and the afterlife awaiting us and on reducing the requirements for the Sabbath** (give rest to those who depend on you, but you yourself can do what you want to do). This is what all the Gospels have in common. And then it will become clear the possibility that Jesus could have been a prophet, that at least **such a possibility cannot be ruled out**. And this is the position of **New Judaism and General Judaism**.

From everything we know about Jesus, it clearly follows: **What he taught does not contradict the basic tenets of the Jewish religion set forth in the Torah and other books of the Old Testament**. This conclusion is supported by an unbiased analysis of the Gospels and many authors writing about Christianity. This is what the same B.V. Pilate writes about Jesus: "He brought the Word into the world, it was a slightly different Word than the one that God told Moses, but one Word did not contradict another Word," "Jesus was in the faith of the fathers." Yes, it certainly was essentially the same Judaism. None of the basic tenets of Judaism were denied by Jesus. The only difference from traditional views, which is not even a difference, but only a completely permissible and, possibly, justified interpretation, is his attitude to the Sabbath: Jesus considered it quite possible to carry out certain activities on the Sabbath, which a person carries according to his will, according to his desire. His words: "Not a man for the Sabbath, but a Sabbath for a man." True, as already mentioned, he often clothed his sermons in a rather sharp, pointed, even sometimes paradoxical form in order to more clearly reveal the essence, to more strongly influence the souls and minds of people, to achieve a change in their views in the right direction. So, for example, realizing that one of the most difficult temptations for the fulfillment of the commandments in this world is the commandment "Do not commit adultery," the violation of which often, it would seem, does not bring any harm to another person and which seems to be not necessary to fulfill, Jesus says: "Everyone who looks at a woman with lust has already committed adultery with her in his heart" (Matthew 5:28), as if this feeling was not given by God, without which it would be impossible to

23

prolong the human race. Of course, this cannot be taken literally. But the strengthening of this commandment is very important, since it protects families from disintegration. Though, in one case, I think, Jesus is clearly wrong: "Whoever divorces his wife not for adultery and marries another commits adultery; and he who marries a divorced woman commits adultery" (Matthew 19: 9). Why is it so with divorced? Why should they remain lonely and unhappy? And how in the case of a clear mistake with the choice of a spouse? Why can't it be fixed? Otherwise, everything is correct. If you are taught that you must turn the other cheek under the blow, this does not mean that you will really turn it up. However, knowing how it should be ideally, people, at least, will not be as angry and quick for revenge and reprisals as they were before this doctrine came into the world. The same applies to the requirement to give up all one's wealth, which is contrary to human nature and in the case of the fulfillment of which the material incentive for any human activity, which is the basis for the development of the economy and all other types of development of society, completely disappears. However, in essence, the teaching of Jesus does not at all contradict the previous provisions of Judaism, but only complements them.

Why did Jesus' disciples and many other people who converted to Christianity think that he was the Messiah? After all, he failed to accomplish what he if he were the Messiah, should have done. Of course, Jesus was an excellent preacher and knew how to heal people, and perhaps, if this is not inventions and exaggerations, and sometimes truly performed miracles. However, there were in those and later times some other people who in this respect were not much inferior to him who also pretended to be the Messiah. Obviously, the decisive factor was the fact of his **resurrection after the execution**, when, three days after it, his body was not found, taken from the cross and left in the cave. This was interpreted as a clear sign of God, proving that Jesus is His true Envoy, resurrected and returned to God. Without this most powerful factor, Christianity would hardly have arisen. According to the Gospels, he also appeared after the resurrection to some people, in particular to his disciples - the 11 apostles and Mary Magdalene.

Unfortunately, **we cannot now confirm or deny the fact of the resurrection of Jesus**, there is a lot of mystery in this matter, and it was too long ago to be able to find out anything now. So, it's a matter of faith. It is possible that the "resurrection" of Jesus, according to Yulia Latynina, was the work of his disciples, who hid his body. But the recognition of Jesus as the Envoy of the Lord does not yet prove that he is the Messiah. After all, he did not fulfill even the very minimum of what was expected of the Messiah, what the Messiah should have done, being the son of the Jewish people, the Envoy of God to him - the liberation of the Jews from Roman rule and poverty. Although Jesus said that he was "sent only to the lost sheep of the house of Israel" (Matthew 15:24). However, after his arrival, the Jews did not fare better, and after a while terrible misfortune fell upon them - the destruction of the Temple, the destruction of a significant part of the people and the next almost two thousand years of exile and scattering in different countries.

So, the fact of Jesus' execution and his subsequent resurrection made a huge impression on everyone who knew him, and subsequently on many other people who received information about these events. However, this did not at all mean the birth of a new religion. Well, the Messiah finally came, he lived among them and taught - it was an extremely exciting event that had a powerful effect on minds. But **his first followers by no means believed that they rejected the faith of the fathers, that their teaching could serve as a source for the birth of a new religion**. As in subsequent times, there were different trends in Judaism at that time. Then they were the Pharisees, Sadducees, Essenes, Zealots. There were considerable

25

differences between them, but they were based on general principles and none of their followers had the idea of declaring this or that direction a new religion. **The ethics and spiritual requirements of Judaism and early Christianity were almost identical.** This is largely indicated by the fact that the highest Jewish clergy did not seriously try to hinder the activities of the first Christian communities. Jesus, the teacher of the early Christians, their Messiah, never spoke of any other faith. He advocated the observance of the laws of the Torah, given to the Jews by God through Moses. As they believed, the Almighty clearly made it clear who Jesus was with the opportunity to perform miracles and the miracle of the resurrection. However, it was necessary to explain why he came, why he went through terrible torments and gave up his earthly life. Is it just to remind you of the need to keep God's commandments and make some additions to them, developing the doctrine of mercy, meekness, non-resistance to evil and clarifying the Sabbath covenant, that is, by and large, not very significant? No, such an explanation did not suit anyone. And then they remembered (unless, of course, this was invented) that Jesus said something not entirely clear that he supposedly had to suffer for people: "The Son of Man came to seek and save what was lost" (Matthew 18:11); "The Son of Man did not come to be served, but to serve and to give His life for the ransom of many" (Matthew 20:28). "Whoever believes and is baptized will be saved; but whoever does not believe will be condemned" (Mark 16:16). Jesus spoke of himself as a Envoy of God who can forgive sins of people and who "must go to Jerusalem ... and be killed, and on the third day rise again" (Matthew 16:21). On this in the Gospels this topic is exhausted, in fact, it is not disclosed in them. Perhaps Jesus himself did not really know about the essence of his mission, he constantly emphasizes that everything he preaches is not from him personally, but from God, that he says what he was told to convey to people. In any case, the mystery of the life and death of Jesus is not revealed in the Gospels. As for baptism, which is literally dedicated to one phrase, the rite

26

of baptism was introduced even before the beginning of the ministry of Jesus and, even more so, before the emergence of Christianity, by John the Baptist, as a symbol of repentance for sins. Their "philosophical schools" developed independently, and many people were baptized with the "baptism of repentance" without even knowing about Jesus.

Thus, on the one hand, **early Christianity was one of the directions of Judaism**, with all the requirements of the latter (circumcision, observance of the requirements of kosher, that is, proper nutrition, and other requirements written in the Torah). It did not lead to a split, and this was its positive quality. On the other hand, the fulfillment of the numerous requirements of Judaism prevented its widespread among other peoples. If for the Jews the fulfillment of these requirements has long been a habit and tradition, then for other peoples, following all the prescriptions of the Torah was very difficult. It was necessary to remove unnecessary obstacles to the wide dissemination of the new teaching. In addition, it was necessary to explain the meaning of the coming of Jesus Christ, his torment. And then a sharp turn took place, resulting in a sharp transformation of early Judeo-Christianity and the gradual formation of a new religion - Christianity: first Messianic Christianity, and then, three hundred years later, after the second sharp turn, traditional Christianity. The author of this first turn is Paul (Saul), who at first was an ardent persecutor of Christians. As a result of his activity, the required explanation of the meaning of the mission of Jesus was given, and obstacles to the spread of Christian teachings among other nations were removed. Unfortunately, this was accomplished by perverting many important tenets of Judaism and early Christianity. But an explanation was required, and it was given.

Paul, who claimed to have had a vision, that he had seen Jesus, then became an extremely ardent champion of faith. However, the current state of the Christian religion did not satisfy him. He developed a new doctrine.

Paul set himself the task of ensuring the widest possible spread of faith in Jesus outside of Judea, among non-Jews. For this, in his opinion, it was necessary to remove all the restrictions imposed by the Jewish religion, except for only the most important provisions regarding faith in the One God - the Creator and in his Son - Jesus Christ. Like other authors of the Bible, being a Jew himself, he, unlike members of the Jerusalem Judeo-Christian community and other first Jewish Christian communities who combined faith in Jesus with Judaism (traditional Judaism), all the requirements of which were sacredly fulfilled, absolutely did not feel the need to observe requirements of Judaism, even many of its most important provisions (at least for non-Jews). Despite the fact that periodically in his writings he speaks about the need to observe the laws given by God; in fact, all of his teaching is aimed at discrediting most of them, at proving the need for strict observance of only those laws that relate to faith in God and in Jesus Christ as His Son, The Envoy and the Messiah; and the need for baptism. Paul broke the thread between Judaism and Christianity. He removed the need to fulfill almost all the requirements recorded in the Torah and other books of the Old Testament, even abandoning circumcision, sacred for the Jews. This was done contrary to clear instructions from Jesus himself about the need for strict observance of the laws given by God. It was precisely because of insufficiently good observance of these laws that he attacked the Jewish priests, accusing them of hypocrisy, i.e., in insufficiently good fulfillment of what they themselves preach, in the slightest deviations from the laws given by the Almighty. There was no talk of any revision of these laws, let alone such a major revision as Paul did. Clearly, Jesus would not approve of this behavior. But **Paul created a new teaching, ignoring the teaching of Jesus Christ.**

These steps of Paul and his practical activities to create new Christian communities outside of Judea led to the widespread spread of Christianity throughout the Roman Empire (and, eventually, throughout the world) in the form of now pure Christianity, without, in fact, the recognition of Judaism as its source, at least the basic laws of which must be followed. As B.V. Pilate writes in the book *The Two Mysteries of Christ* (Chapter 21, p. 230), "The mighty spirit of monotheism, engendered by her (Judea - author's note), cried out invitingly into the world. And the huge Roman Empire heard his call. She shuddered and, like a midwife, carefully took into her arms the newborn baby - Christianity." Thus, on the one hand, largely due to the work of Paul, "the teaching of Jesus" began to spread widely across the planet. All obstacles to this have been removed. On the other hand, apart from the belief in the One God from the underlying religion, from what Jesus himself preached, almost nothing remained. It was already a completely different religion. It was based on Paul's change of the essence, the spiritual basis of Judaism and early Christianity so much that their combination with the new Christianity became almost impossible. These were - the rejection of the requirements of the Torah and Paul's announcement of the priority of faith over the deeds of man, before the fulfillment of all the laws of the Most High that are not directly related to faith in him, including even those that were given by God by his Basic Law - the Ten Commandments. Paul argued that only by faith can a person be saved, and the way a person lives, his whole life, all his good and bad deeds, the fulfillment or non-fulfillment of God's commandments relating to how a person should live - all this supposedly does not have the main , of decisive importance, equal to faith. "No one is justified by the law before God, - this is clear, because the righteous will live by faith" (Galatians 3: 10-11). "Man is justified before God by faith alone, apart from the works of the Law" (Romans 3:28). "If salvation can be achieved by good deeds, then there is no point in crucifying Christ. Christ, therefore, sacrificed his life in vain" (Galatians 2:21). Ideology, philosophical views of a person were placed higher than his specific activity throughout his life. If you believe, went through the baptism ceremony, symbolizing faith in Jesus (even soon after birth, as is usually done, when a person still does not understand what it is, or even by force, against the will of a person), then you can atone for sins and be saved despite all the sins. Paul rejected circumcision and kosher. All of this was in stark contrast to early Christianity and Judaism, as well as to what Jesus himself taught. In particular, one of the prophets of Judaism, Jeremiah, wrote: "Behold, the days are coming," the Lord said, "when ... they will no longer say: 'the fathers ate the unripe fruit, but the children's teeth are set on edge,' and everyone will die for his guilt" (31: 26-30).

Here is what Solomon Dinkevich writes in the book *Jews, Judaism, Israel*: "Christianity owes its transformation into an independent religion to the activity of the Apostle Paul. Paul put forward a concept that allowed him to renounce the Torah. Judaism claims that a person's deeds are higher than his faith, it is deeds, good and bad, that are the criterion for his assessment. In the book of King Shlomo (Solomon) "Kohelet" (7:20) we read: "There is no such righteous man on Earth who would do good and would not sin." For this reason, Judaism provides a person with the opportunity to commit "teshuva" - to repent of committed sins and return to God. However, Paul denied this - see above the Epistle to Galatians 2:21 and others. Paul bases his concept of denial of the Torah on the verse from the Fifth Book of the Torah (Deut. 27:26): "Cursed is he who does not fulfill the words of this teaching" (i.e., does not keep the commandments of the Torah). This verse is explained in the Oral Torah: it is about punishment from Heaven (by means of a curse) for a serious violation of the laws of the Torah in a situation where a human court is powerless to punish the guilty person, for example, for murder without witnesses. Ignoring or not knowing this explanation, Paul argued that since there are no sinless people, it clearly follows from the above verse that every person from his very birth is already cursed by Heaven. The death of Jesus, he said, became "a sacrifice before God for all believers (in Jesus) and for all time." Thus, Paul replaced the Torah with faith in Jesus Christ: "Christ redeemed us from the curse of the Law, becoming a curse for us" (Galatians 3:13). Initially, Christians say, the Jews were God's Chosen People, but refusing to recognize Jesus as the Son of God, they were rejected. Now we - Christians have become the chosen people, and all the rest are doomed to the torments of hell. However, as Adin Steinsaltz noted, "if Yeshua were resurrected, he would rather go to the synagogue than to the church, which he would mistake for a pagan temple." Like Jesus, all his disciples were Jewish, and the original Christian sect consisted of a small number of Jews. Making sure that the Jews did not respond to his calls, Paul turned all his attention to the Gentiles and, wishing to simplify and facilitate their conversion to Christianity, replaced circumcision with baptism - dipping into a font: "Here I am, Paul, I tell you: if you are circumcised, then Christ will be of no use to you" (Galatians 5: 2). An independent history of Christianity began. Paul's proclaimed 'priority of faith over works' gave rise to missionary work, including forcible conversion by the cross and sword, and later the 'judgment of faith' - the Holy Inquisition."

What did this approach lead to? It actually meant that, not to mention all the other requirements of the Almighty, even instead of the sacred, dictated by Himself and absolutely obligatory for the fulfillment of the Ten Commandments, **only the first one remained obligatory, talking about the One God and the inadmissibility of other gods** - well, as a maximum, the first three, i.e., the first additions concerning the prohibition of images and sculptures (which no one ever observes, and especially among the followers of Christianity, using numerous icons of Jesus, the Virgin Mary and many saints) and mentioning the name of God in vain (which is also not observed). And this only First Commandment also turned out to be very shaken, because **Jesus Christ became the object of worship along with**

God. Subsequently, this even allowed him to be declared God Himself, His inseparable part. The same important commandments as "do not kill, do not steal, do not commit adultery, do not desire (do not take away) ... anything that is from your neighbor, do not speak false testimony about your neighbor, honor your father and your mother" how a person should live, in fact, have been relegated to the level of non-binding. This became the ideological, spiritual basis for the subsequent cruel massacres, tortures, Jewish pogroms and expulsions, the Inquisition, the Crusades, and the silence of the Christian Church during the monstrous genocides of the Jewish people, carried out by Hitler and many others before him, not to mention the terrible persecutions and murders in the Middle Ages, directly inspired by the church. And almost all of this was done in the name of Jesus, for his glory. But to the direct question – "What can I do good in order to have eternal life?" Jesus replied, "Do not kill; do not commit adultery; do not steal; do not bear false witness; honor father and mother; and: love your neighbor as yourself." Who has the right to correct Jesus? And why should we trust such "rulers" and not Jesus himself? This and other similar sayings of Jesus express the very essence of Judaism. Those who believe in Jesus must understand: **Jesus preached nothing more than Judaism, strict observance of its laws**, and some exaggeration of some of its provisions by Jesus or the introduction of some new approaches on certain issues was not of a fundamental nature, did not touch the essence of Judaism.

It is striking that the sharp turn made by Paul went almost unnoticed, as if it did not exist. The case is presented as if early Christianity as a branch of Judaism never existed, as if it immediately arose in the form that Paul made it. Although historians are well aware of what sharp, irreconcilable contradictions existed between Paul and the leader of the first, Jerusalem, Christian community, Peter, and other members of this community. Then followed a sharp break between Peter and Paul. As B.V. Pilate writes, "The difference in the views of the schools was so great that their break was inevitable." The brother of Jesus, James, who led the community after Peter, was even more "conservative" than the liberal Peter, who considered it possible to introduce some concessions for the pagans, since he considered the spread of Judeo-Christianity (Christian Judaism) to be the will of God, but, of course, while maintaining its main provisions without changing its essence, as Paul did. For Peter, as well as for Mark, Matthew, Luke, John (the authors of the Gospels), James and other members of the first community, what Paul did was sacrilege. He was like from another world to them. His speeches terrified them. Here is what B.V. Pilate, the namesake of the procurator of Judea Pontius Pilate, writes about them in his magnificent book *The Two Mysteries of Christ*: "In fact, their religion was the same Judaism, which contained the idea that Jesus was the Messiah. The first Christian communities were based on Jewish, and the breakup was not easy for them. Unfortunately, most of the communities followed Paul, the rest eventually melted into Judaism. Attempts to spread early Christianity widely failed. The result was the absolute oblivion of true history and the substitution of false doctrine for primordial Christianity. After all, the teaching of Paul is presented by the church fathers as the teaching of Jesus Christ." It would seem that an amazing substitution should be striking to everyone who has read the Gospels and the main works of Paul. But, oddly enough, this does not happen. Most Christians live in the confidence that they are spiritual followers of Jesus Christ. True, recently there has been a process of restoring the prestige of fulfilling at least the Ten Commandments. But this is not enough. Sooner or later, all the i's must be officially dotted, and the lie must be exposed. Then, I hope, the truth will become obvious to everyone, just as it is obvious to me, and we can return to the sources that are closer to the Truth.

33

Jesus never said that he was God and repeatedly turned to God with prayer. And during the first hundreds of years of Christianity's existence, no one considered him God, and the Holy Trinity was invented later. And if Jesus is not God Himself, but His Envoy, even the Son, then worshiping him, praying in front of his images and the very making of such images is a serious violation of one of the Ten Commandments of God (the second commandment), - do not create an idol for yourself, Therefore, - no "incarnations," otherwise this commandment would have no meaning, since worship of the one who is considered the Envoy of God, could always be explained by the fact that we consider him "the embodiment of the One God," a "part" of Him.

Jesus never said that he was called to remove from people some kind of curse of God (and also about original sin, in general about such a concept). If this was his mission, why did he never talk about it himself, why did he not preach what then formed the basis of Christianity? No, Jesus fought for people to fulfill the commandments of God set forth in the Torah and other books of the Old Testament. It turns out that **Christians**, for whom Jesus is an idol, and for the majority God Himself, **do not follow his teachings, but listen to others, subsequent authors, and, accordingly, belong to a different religion, not at all to the one to which Jesus himself referred and fought for the observance of the laws**. Most Christians, influenced by Christian preachers, sincerely believe that they are following "the teaching of Christ."

Of course, many things coincide, especially in recent Christianity - it is now significantly different from what it was in the Middle Ages. Like Judaism and each of the humanistic religions, it, as a rule, performs the most important function of educating people in a spirit of love for each other and for fulfilling the main commandments of God, which essentially coincide with humanism, with universal human morality. In fact, most of its trends, like Judaism, teach kindness and mercy. Although Christianity has softer specific requirements for people in this sense, especially with regard to the question of the possibility of receiving forgiveness for their sins. No one denies that the God of Christians is also the God of the Jews. In fact, a group of Jews managed to force almost half of the earthly population to believe in a Jewish God. The process of significant changes in Christianity in the modern era should in no case be stopped, for this process means its gradual movement towards strengthening its humane component and the embodiment of God's commandments.

However, according to a number of basic signs, this is completely different from what Jesus preached. After all, the recognition of Jesus as God, who allegedly delivered those who underwent the rite of baptism from the curse of original sin and opened the way for them to paradise, and the accusation of executing Jesus, i.e., those positions that in earlier times served as the ideological basis for centuries of repression and murder, in some leading directions of Christianity continue to persist. I think **Jesus himself would have been amazed to learn how much of what he taught was transformed. If people really followed his teachings, this could never lead to such a monstrous paradox of history that the representatives of Christianity tortured and killed Jesus' fellow tribesmen - the Jews**, who created this religion, and even now many hate them. To justify the bloody massacres of Jews, they raised monstrous and unjust accusations of killing Christian babies for the ritual use of their blood, although the Jewish religion forbids human sacrifice; many generations of Jews were blamed for the alleged complicity of their distant ancestors in the execution of Jesus (only in 1965 the Catholic Church dropped this charge against the Jews), etc. I wonder what Jesus himself would have said about all of this? How can this be combined with the worship of a Jew - Jesus?

I propose to follow the **commandments of God written in the Torah** and other books of the Old Testament, and the teaching of Jesus that is in line with them, i.e., **what Jesus himself preached**. This is the only thing that the true religion should consist of, corresponding to the wishes and commandments of the Creator. Although strict proofs are impossible in religion, an unbiased analysis of history inevitably leads to this conclusion. However, perhaps the right way is to fulfill the requirements set forth in the Torah, which apply to all people. This would significantly expand the circle of followers while maintaining the basics. Kirk Douglas said: "As I studied the Torah, I realized that God does not need our praises. He wants only one thing from us - that we become better." And the more people understand this and join a righteous life, the better. In other words, what Paul was doing, i.e., the spread of Judaism, adjusted for use by all the peoples of the Earth, is also very important, you just need to get rid of the mistakes he made.

Here we will make a small excursion into the past. A lot is confusing in the generally accepted concept of the execution of Jesus, which blames the Jews for it in the first place and assigns to its direct perpetrators, the Romans, the role of executors of their will. For example, it is known that the procurator of Judea, Pontius Pilate, was the first initiator of the persecution of Jesus, who exerted the strongest pressure on the supreme clergy of the Jews, which actually determined their subsequent behavior. Here is what B.V. Pilate writes about this in the book *The Two Mysteries of Christ* (Chapter 36, pp. 402-404): "On the eve of Easter, Jesus enters Jerusalem. Thousands of people welcome him. "The whole city began to move and they said: Who is this? And the people said: This is Jesus, the Prophet from Nazareth of Galilee" (Matthew 21:10, 11). The crowd is becoming more and more exalted. Both the Roman and Jewish authorities must, simply must, treat this phenomenon with increasing alarm. A few days before this, to the question "Is it permissible to give a tribute to Caesar or not?" Jesus answered ambiguously: "Give back to Caesar what is Caesar's, and what is God's to God." The correctness of the answer is far from obvious, especially for a Roman official. For himself, he makes one thing: "The state will not receive a part of the income." Moreover, this phrase was spoken in public. Its provocative. It smells of sulfur, because even an indirect appeal not to pay taxes is certainly approved by the Jews, and it can lead to unrest ... Jesus constantly gathers a huge audience around him. Pilgrims begin to flock to the city, their number grows, and the number of Jesus' listeners increases accordingly. On Thursday, Pilate summons Caiaphas (the high priest), possibly other members of the Jewish elite, and says the following: "Rabbi, I called you in order to express concern about your inaction. Your young preacher, with your connivance and love of discussion, gathers a huge number of admirers, and from his sermons he brings rebellion. And I am an old campaigner and I feel rebellion for many days. We Romans are aware of your relationship to the authority of Caesar. After the death of Herod, the joyful mood of the crowd, without any reason, grew into a revolt against the Romans. It happened, if you remember, on Easter. I do not want blood at all, neither yours, nor, in particular, Roman, I have seen too much of it, but it is my duty to warn you that if measures are not taken, then any public speeches will be brutally suppressed." The Jews bow out. Caiaphas is urgently calling a meeting. He reports to the assembly what Pilate said. He ends his speech with a phrase that any of the high priests of Judea could safely subscribe to: "It is better for one person to die for the people." Thus, the behavior of the Jewish elite was forced - it proceeded from the desire to prevent numerous victims and was dictated by the Romans, in particular by Pilate. All further behavior of the latter, his alleged reluctance at first to execute Jesus was only posturing and a desire to absolve himself of guilt. And from the point of view of the believer: If God decided that the execution of Jesus was inevitable, that "this cup" could not escape him, then, naturally, all the participants in this drama could not act differently, contrary to the desire of God Himself, their corresponding behavior was programmed, otherwise the execution of Jesus could not take place. Therefore, blaming someone in this case is simply pointless. An indicator of this is the fact that the Jewish court, the Sanhedrin, in the entire history of its existence, has passed only one death sentence - for actions that we would now call terrorism. Crucifixion could not have been a method of execution at all. And the Romans during their rule in Judea executed a huge number of its inhabitants by crucifixion. In addition, such facts raise doubts. What could have forced Pilate to leave the palace several times to listen to the opinion of the "Jewish crowd?" Why did he wash his hands in front of this crowd, saying that he did not have the blood of Jesus on him, although this was a purely Jewish custom, absolutely not typical of the Romans? All of this suggests that the facts in the Gospels were fabricated.

There is also another version. Here is what Arie Baraz writes: "In many historical studies, instead of an atmosphere of seething political discontent, we are painted with a picture of a peaceful Roman province. Many Bible scholars and independent scholars are convinced that the Gospels are not a "reliable source" in everything related to the judgment of Jesus. Writer Baigent Michael: "In that era, they were sentenced to crucifixion for political crimes. According to the testimony of the Gospel, Pilate put the fate of Jesus into the hands of the crowd, which demanded crucifixion. According to the laws of Judea, the punishment for such a crime was stoning. Crucifixion is a Roman execution that was sentenced for incitement to rebellion." Jesus was sentenced to death for political crimes. The first violin in this trial was played by the Romans, not the authorities of Judea. Professor Samuel Brandon: "The movement associated with Jesus bore at least some resemblance to rebellion, so that the Romans in it a possible rebel and executed him on this charge." Research by Chaim Cohen

"Jesus. Judgment and Crucifixion" shows that the priests were on the side of Jesus, that the meeting of the "Sanhedrin" they had started was an attempt to shield the Teacher. They deliberately tried to discover the "lack of evidence" to testify in a Roman court that the charges against Jesus were absurd. Cohen explains the exclamation "guilty of death" as a statement of fact: now, after Jesus himself openly proclaimed himself king, he will be condemned by the Roman court. It is impossible to save him. "The claim of a mortal man to be parallel to the emperor, and even more so to an exclusive title, was unacceptable." The man proclaimed by the Messiah was a "blasphemer" in the eyes of Rome, not Jerusalem. In Jerusalem he was honored as a hero. "For thousands of years, the Jews have been indulged in fire and sword because their ancestors were guilty of the death of Jesus, while they did everything humanly possible to save him from the Roman executioners." The drama of the Gospel is based on the fact that God was rejected by His chosen people: the death sentence of the Messiah is passed by the Jewish High Priest. But the religious and historical context testifies that the trial of the "King of the Jews" could have been initiated only by Pilate.

About hell in its traditional Christian understanding. **There can be no eternal punishment**, while a person's entire life lasts on average seventy to eighty years, this is too cruel and contrary to elementary justice and all the commandments of the Almighty, which are imbued with the spirit of goodness, love, and mercy. I will repeat again and again: it is impossible to even imagine eternal torment, without any opportunity to ever atone for your sins. And for God to doom people to this? No, it is impossible, unjustified, and even sinful to suspect the Lord of such cruelty - this position is clearly untenable. Hell can only be a **temporary** punishment before heaven (purgatory). And we cannot say for sure that Jesus spoke specifically about the **eternal paradise**. Perhaps this, too, was attributed to him by the authors of the Gospels. The fact that eternal hell awaits many, and only by baptism and faith in Jesus can one be saved from it, gave rise (along with, of course, the increased aggressiveness of representatives of Christianity caused by the desire to expand their sphere of influence) to the desire to baptize everyone in a row, which took extremely violent forms in the Middle Ages, and the opportunity to atone for sins and be saved by faith gave birth to and generates new sinners. Over time, most of the Messianic Judaism created by the Jews, through the efforts of Paul, turned into Messianic Christianity, and then it turned into modern Christianity, which considers Jesus to be God, which so departed from Judaism that the Torah was pushed aside by subsequent books of the New Testament, and the followers of Judaism are Jews, fellow tribesmen of Jesus. were subjected to pogroms and persecution. A huge number of them fell victim to Christians who allegedly acted under the banner of Jesus Christ. The Jews, even on pain of death, refused to accept such a religion. This would mean disobeying the Creator's direct demand for them not to create idols for themselves, not to worship false gods. Moreover, with the name of this false god, they were persecuted and killed, violating the most important God's commandments and thereby, **convincingly confirming the falsity of this religion**.

Most Christians are well aware that **God bequeathed Palestine to the Jews.** They remember the words of the Most High: "For behold, in those days and at that time, when I restore Judah and Jerusalem from exile, I will gather all nations and bring them down to the valley of Jehoshaphat. I will plead[a] with them there **on behalf of My people, even My inheritance, Israel, whom they scattered among the nations, and they divided up My land**" (Joel 4: 1-3). In other words, the **destruction of the Jews as a people threatens with innumerable calamities for all of humanity. I think most Christians should understand this.** Britain received a mandate to the land bequeathed to the Jews by God to create a Home for the Jewish people here. It was created against her wishes, perhaps by the will of God, it was like a miracle. And it shouldn't be destroyed.

INJUDAISM

So, an unbiased analysis of Jesus' activities shows that he was preaching precisely Judaism, addressed to the Jews, with all its high demands set forth in the Torah, and nothing else, moreover, its Pharisaic version, i.e., faith, along with faith in the One and Indivisible God, in the afterlife. Further natural development of theological thought went in two directions: in relation to Jesus Christ and in the number of the requirements of God necessary for believers to fulfill. Let's start with the second one. Here is my view on which commandments should be fulfilled by non-Jews.

As I already wrote, it cannot be ruled out that, perhaps, for non-Jews, the right way is to fulfill the requirements set forth in the Torah, **which apply to all people, and not just to Jews**. This would significantly expand the circle of followers while maintaining the basics. And there are many such commandments. Here are **the current commandments of the Torah** and, accordingly, **the Bible** as a whole, which **apply to all people**, and not only to Jews, and not to priests who already know them (many commandments do not work now because there is no Temple or they are outdated, for example, they mention peoples that do not exist now). This is the minimum. That is, each of the believers is free to choose - to fulfill all the commandments of the Torah or only those listed below. Here are the commandments that must be followed:

Ten Commandments: "Do not kill. Don't steal. Do not covet your neighbor's house; do not covet your neighbor's wife, nor his servant, nor his bull, nor his donkey, nor anything that is with your neighbor. Do not speak false testimony of your neighbor. Honor your father and your mother, so that your days on Earth may be prolonged. Do not commit adultery. Remember the sabbath day - work six days and do all your work, but on the seventh day, sabbath, do no work, neither you, nor your son, nor your daughter, nor your servant, nor your servant girl, nor your cattle. (If Jesus is indeed a prophet, then the strictness of the Sabbath observance requirement is greatly reduced. His words: "Not a man for the Sabbath, but a Sabbath for a man." This is the only significant change in the commandments brought by Jesus. That is, give rest to those who it depends on you, but you can do something yourself if you really want it - author's note)."

Other commandments of the Torah:

"God is one. Love Him and be afraid. Sanctify His Name. Do not defile the Name of God. Do not allow the thought that there are other gods besides the Most High. Thank God. Serve Him. To become like the Almighty in His actions. Do not blaspheme. Taking an oath in His Name. Do not curse and defile the Name of the Most High, do not question the promises and warnings of God expressed by the prophet, do not destroy the houses of serving God, do not destroy the books of the prophets. To dedicate the firstborn to God.

Do not create statues and images for worship, do not make idols and do not worship them, do not serve them and do not call, do not tempt to serve them. Do not prophesy in the name of an idol. Do not engage in idolatry or study it. Do not make cult obelisks and stone floorings for prostration worship. It is forbidden to swear by the name of an idol. Do not use anything related to idolatry. Do not hand over your children to serve Molech (pagan deities). Forbidding the tempted to serve idols to love the tempter. Do not forgive, do not save, do not justify the tempter. Don›t benefit from idol jewelry. Do not make an alliance with idolaters, do not marry idolaters, do not be merciful to them.

Not to pronounce the Name of God in vain. To confess aloud to the Almighty in any sin. Fulfill all vows taken. Do not swear in vain, do not break the words of the oath, do not break your obligations. Teach Torah and teach it to others. Do not change anything in the Torah. Respect sages, Torah scholars. Strive to communicate with them. To love a hera (a person who converted to Judaism). Do not prophesy falsely and do not listen to the words of a false prophet, do not tremble before him. Do not allow ideas that contradict the worldview of the Torah. Obey the true prophets.

Build and honor and guard the Temple. Come to the Temple (synagogue, prayer house - author›s note) during the holidays. Celebrate holidays in the Temple. A ban on entering the Temple or teaching Torah while drunk.

Do not kill each other, do not kill a criminal without trial and investigation. Execute for specific crimes. Separate those guilty of manslaughter. Do not leave a person in mortal danger.

Do not rob. Do not kidnap people, money and property. Do not take over what belongs to others. Do not deny the debts you owe. Do not delay payment of debt. Do not deceive each other in trade, in transactions. Comply with the laws of purchase and sale. Do not swear falsely by denying your debts. Don't cheat. Do not keep in your possession the wrong weights and other measuring instruments. Do not disregard a thing lost by someone. Return the lost to its owner.

Do not shy away from providing material assistance to the poor. Support the poor. Lend to the poor. Do not demand the repayment of the debt if it is known that the debtor is not able to repay it. Do not take a pledge from a debtor by force, do not take a pledge from a widow. The prohibition of the debtor to withhold the pledge at the hour when the lender needs it.

Do not inflict beatings. Do not spread gossip and slander. The prohibition to hate each other, to show vindictiveness. Do not take revenge on each other, do not shame each other, do not curse. To save the hunted from the killer chasing him. Do not let each other down with unscrupulous advice. Do not offend each other with speeches, do not insult, do not curse, do not oppress widows and orphans. Love your neighbor as yourself.

Create a fair judicial system. Appoint judges and bailiffs. Ensure the equality of the parties in court. Consider a litigation between the prosecutor and the defendant. Give testimony before the court. Check the testimony of witnesses. Prohibiting a judge from administering an unjust trial, accepting gifts, treating one of the parties with partiality, passing an acquittal out of fear of a criminal or out of pity in favor of a poor man, judging a person with a bias, showing leniency towards someone who killed unintentionally, listening to the claims of one of the parties in the absence of the other , to make a decision, relying only on the opinion and authority of another judge, to impose such punishments that can lead to death, to accept a ransom for the criminal who committed premeditated murder. Do not impose a death sentence if there is only one vote. Do not testify perjury, do not accept testimony from a wicked person or relatives, do not accept a verdict based on the words of one witness. Do not punish someone who has been forced into a crime. Warn and reproach the perpetrator of a misdemeanor or one who intends to commit one. Prohibiting a witness from expressing his opinion on the case where he is a witness. Do not spare the life of the persecutor. Follow the majority in case of voting.

Respect your parents, tremble in front of them, do not beat them.

To be fruitful and multiply, to strive for procreation. Take care of children. Do not take your young husband away from home in the first year after the wedding. Not to enter into intimacy with the mother, with the sister, with the father›s wife, with the father›s daughter from another wife, with the daughter, with the daughter of the son, with the daughter of the wife, with the granddaughter, with the granddaughter of the wife, with the sister of the father or mother, with the wife of the son, with brother›s wife, father›s brother›s wife, with his wife›s sister during her lifetime, with her father, with her father›s brother. Do not commit adultery (in the "soft" interpretation "do not change" - author's note): Do not enter into intimacy with a woman without a marriage contract, with a married woman. Do not intercourse between a man and another man. Do not get close to animals. The rapist is obliged to marry the woman he has raped. Do not show signs of intimacy in relation to persons with whom intimacy is prohibited. It is forbidden to divorce a wife if the husband falsely stated that he did not find traces of virginity on her.

A person who touches the corpse of an animal or is struck by tsaraat (leprosy), his clothes, house, as well as a woman in labor who is flowing mucus, a dead person transmit ritual impurity (tumu). To get rid of all types of tuma, you need to plunge into a mikveh (water tank). Observe the laws of evaluating a person, "unclean" animals, houses, fields. Do not enter into intimacy with the ritually impure (tame).

Do not do work on Saturday or holidays. Rest. (If Jesus is indeed a prophet, then the strictness of the Sabbath-keeping requirement is greatly reduced. This is the one of the Ten Commandments that causes the most rejection among non-Jews, and the only significant change brought by Jesus - author's note).

Do not harass an employee by delaying his salary. Do not load a slave (employee) with meaningless work. It is forbidden for an employee to eat during work or to take with him fruits from the field or garden in which he works. An employee can eat from the fruits that he processes.

Keep track of months and years.

Do not cultivate or harvest the land in the seventh year and in the fiftieth year.

Do not engage in magic, divination, astrology, do not turn to a fortuneteller, do not believe in omens, do not call the souls of the dead, do not go to the one who summons the souls of the dead, do not wear clothes of the opposite sex.

Do not leave sources of increased danger in settlements and houses. Make fences on roofs, around pits, etc.

Do not leave without the help of a traveler whose beast of burden fell.

Do not cross between different types of animals. Prohibition to castrate. Send a mother bird from the nest if you want to take eggs or chicks. Do not take poultry together with chicks or eggs.

Forbid the king to increase his personal treasury. Observe the rules of waging war with other peoples. Do not be afraid of the enemy during the war."

There are about 200 commandments, let's call them the **Commandments of Injudaism**. And a religion that coincides with Judaism in relation to Jesus Christ but considers it sufficient to fulfill the above commandments and does not have a rigid connection between nationality and religion, like Judaism, let us call **Injudaism** (International Judaism, Intranational Judaism). I think that **the fulfillment of these commandments is enough for non-Jews and should be the general minimum for all religions based on faith in the One God.**

However, for those who want to become a **Judaist** in the traditional sense of the word, i.e. a follower of Judaism, this is almost enough. Following the Torah completely is not easy. To do this, you need to study it well. This is not required of most Judaists; rather superficial knowledge

is enough. In fact, in addition to the knowledge of the previous commandments, the following is required:

Get circumcised.

Not to work and fast on Yom Kippur (Yom Ha Kipurim) - Judgment
Day, 10th Tishrei, the day of repentance and absolution, when the fate of a
person is decided on the New Year. Do not work on the first day and on the
seventh day of Passover, on Rosh Hashanah, on the first day of Sukkot, on
Shemini Atzeret, on Shapuot (Passover is a holiday in honor of the exodus
from Egypt, Rosh Hashanah is the Jewish New Year, Sukkot - a holiday in
memory of wandering in the Sinai desert, Shemini Atzeret - the 8th last
day of the holiday of Sukkot, Shavuot - the Day of the gift of the Torah).
Live in the Sukkah and rejoice in front of the Almighty for seven days of
the Sukkot holiday. All people gather on the second day of Sukkot at the
end of every seventh year to read the Torah. Light candles before Shabbat.

Do not eat the meat of "unclean" cattle and "unclean" wild animals, fish
and birds (especially the meat of a pig that eats its excrement - author's
note). Do not eat insects and reptiles. Don't eat carrion. Do not eat flesh cut
from a live animal. Check for signs of kosher in livestock, animals, birds,
and fish. Do not eat what has become unfit for eating. Do not eat blood. Do
not cook meat in milk, do not eat meat cooked in milk. Do not eat meat
and dairy products together. Do not be a glutton and a drunkard.

In other words, it is enough to honor and celebrate Jewish holidays,
the Sabbath, circumcise (for men, usually male infants) and follow the
basic rules of kosher nutrition. In total, it is enough to observe about 225 of
the above commandments, let's call them the **minimum commandments
of a Judaist.**

48

JUDAISM, PROFETISM, INVOISM, MESSIAN CHRISTIANITY

Now about the differences according to another main characteristic, for those who believe in God, it depends on the attitude towards Jesus Christ.

1. The existing "basic" religion **Judaism**. Source: The main part of the Bible - from its beginning to the Gospels, i.e., Torah and books of the prophets. Belief in the One God - the Creator and that God requires people to comply with the laws set forth in the Torah. Neither the Envoy of God (nor, moreover, God Himself as part of the Trinity), nor the prophet, Jesus Christ is recognized. Our future is determined only by the One and Indivisible God. The need to fulfill all the covenants of God given in the Torah, a part of the Bible given by God through Moses. At least the fulfillment of 225 commandments of a Jewish Jew. Connection with nationality - a follower of Judaism is considered a Jew. To accept Judaism, non-Jews need to go through conversion. History shows that Jews must abide by the main commandments and not switch to other, hostile to them, religions, otherwise they will be punished. Those. such Judaism unites all currents of **Judaism**, strictly associated with the Jewish nationality. It is hardly surprising that the Jews do not recognize Jesus Christ, in whose name they were repeatedly persecuted, humiliated, and killed for many centuries. And some of his statements, cited in the Gospels, cannot but cause mistrust. The only option that can inspire confidence in at least his main theses,

which are repeated in all the Gospels, is that he did not leave any notes and could be distorted by their authors. However, in any case, the influence of Jesus undoubtedly affected Judaism, the final "victory" of the Pharisees over the Sadducees was won, i.e., supporters of the existence of an afterlife over their opponents.

As I already wrote above, in my opinion, there should also be a new, missionary (in all countries except Israel) religion **Injudaism** (International Judaism, Brot Judaism, Wide Judaism, International Judaism, Soft Judaism, Basic Judaism), which considers it necessary to fulfill at least the Ten Commandments and a number (approximately 200) of the Injuda Commandments taken from the Torah that apply to all people on Earth. And also, **Light-Injudaism**, in addition to this, interpreting the prohibition of adultery as a prohibition of only adultery, and also allowing drawing - just do not make an idol out of what is drawn, i.e., with the exception of those images that can cause the idolization of the depicted (in particular, Jesus Christ). **The connection with nationality here and further (for all religions, except for Judaism and General Judaism) may be absent, while all obstacles to their spread are removed and they acquire, in contrast to Judaism, a missionary character.**

2. The existing "basic" religion of **Prophetism** (Prophet-Injudaism or In-Prophetism), which differs from Judaism in **the recognition of Jesus as one of the prophets** (prophet - prophet in English), as well as in the democratic choice of whether to fulfill all the commandments or the main 200 and the fact that it may not be associated with nationality and is a common missionary religion. Requirements for keeping the Sabbath are reduced - as Jesus said, "not a man for the Sabbath, but a Sabbath for a man." In other words, a person should have at least one day off from work a week, Saturday, and give rest on that day to those who depend on him but can choose for himself what to do on that day. I have called prophetism in

an enlarged manner, based on the main criterion. Of the existing religions, it includes the Socinianists (there are few of them left) and a significant or even most of the Unitarians. Both recognize Jesus as a man - a prophet of God and do not recognize the concept of "original sin," and therefore do not consider Jesus' mission as an atoning sacrifice. There may also be **Prophet-Judaism** (Judaism-Prophetism), for those who consider it necessary to fulfill all the commandments of the Torah or the minimum 225 commandments necessary for a Jew-Judaist, i.e., differing from traditional Judaism only by the recognition of Jesus as a prophet. I think that the inclusion of Jesus among the prophets without his idolization at this stage will not harm Judaism but will only increase the number of its adherents. This is analogous to the inclusion of Buddha among the prophets of Hinduism and the inclusion of Jesus among the prophets of Islam. Both religions have only benefited from this.

3. The existing "basic" religion (EBR) is **Messianic Christianity** (Messianism), again, taken on a large scale, according to the main postulates. Among the existing religions, it includes, in particular, **Jehovah's Witnesses**, partly **Unitarianism** (Unitarianism, Unitarianism), the Philippine **Church of Christ** and some other branches of **Protestantism** that reject the Trinity. The source is the entire Bible. Jesus Christ is recognized as the Messiah - created by God and foretold by the prophets as a special Envoy and Son of God, for whom this was the first coming and who will come to people, i.e. he is recognized as the Messiah - the Savior who must come to Earth in the future to transform our world for the better - but not by God Himself (that is, the Trinity is not recognized as an option). According to this religion (a group of religions), God will make the Jews accept Jesus, everything is in His power (just as He provided, when He considered it necessary, the execution of Jesus). In particular, Jesus can confess that he already came to Earth under the Name of Jesus (Yeshua), only after

51

completing his mission. Messianic Judaism believes that you can only pray to God, not to Jesus. The virgin birth is recognized. For the Judaists, there is **Messianic Judaism** (Judeo-Christianity), which coincides with Primary Christianity, which in the first century was part of Judaism. He considers it necessary to fulfill all the commandments of God given in the Torah, or at least 225 main commandments of the Judaist.

4. New "base" religion **Invoism** - filling the "blank spot" in the base religions between Prophetism and Messianic Christianity. It differs from the latter in that Jesus Christ is recognized as the Envoy of God, the Son of God, but not the Messiah - the Savior who must come and bring peace and prosperity to Earth. He had another function, only preparing such a parish for the future Messiah - by initiating the creation and widespread dissemination of the monotheistic movement. He is not the only Son of God (otherwise he probably would have said this) and will not be sent to Earth a second time, since he must come to the Jews, and the Jews will clearly not accept him after two thousand years of murder, bullying, forced baptisms, and persecutions done with his name on the lips. Yes, he did not promise this - he promised to come to **his contemporaries** and did not come. All texts of the Bible are respected, but considering the subsequent earthly history and, accordingly, the understanding of the impossibility of the coming of Jesus Christ to earth. That is, Jesus, with all due respect to his feats, is history. He is also not connected with nationality and is a missionary religion. He considers it necessary to fulfill, at least, the commandments of the Torah addressed to all people, i.e., Ten Commandments and 200 Commandments of Injudaism (see above). Another version of it is **Invoy-Judaism** (Judaism-Invoism, Invo-Judaism, Judeo-Invoism), - for those who consider it necessary to fulfill all the commandments of the Torah or the minimum required 225.

UNIFYING RELIGIONS

When one gets acquainted with existing religions, it is surprising that there is only one "unifying" religion (Baha'ism), while such a unifying religion should be generated by each of the "basic" religions, starting with the second. This prompted me to try to create an aggregated, generalized picture of existing and potential religions (see below). But at the moment I will cite only those religions that are **based on faith in the One God** and, in my opinion, can correspond to the truth, because reject only one option, that Jesus is God Himself or a part of Him (part of the Trinity). This is what the Christian theologian Yuri Lutsenko writes: "Pluralism has a strong side in that it calls for the peaceful acceptance of any non-aggressive ideas and opinions. Unfortunately, adherents of different views are guided not by rapprochement or at least respect, but by isolation, based on the belief in the correctness of exclusively their views. Very often the consciousness is ruled by fanaticism - the result of blind faith and its indispensable companion - aggression." There is no complete knowledge yet. This shows the need for the existence of **unifying** religions, each of which "accommodates" a number of similar views. These religions can be called unifying or conditional. They are not divided depending on how the afterlife is represented by a particular religion (since sometimes there are different ideas about this within one religion). The division goes only **depending on the attitude towards Jesus Christ and on the number and list of commandments**

necessary for fulfilling (common to all 200 commandments of the Torah, 225 commandments, which are the minimum for Judaists, 613 commandments of the Torah from the list of Maimonides, or all commandments of the Torah). Each of them, as a rule, unites several close religions. In fact, these are not religions, but groups of similar religions, united according to main characteristics. This makes it easier to navigate the sea of religions. In particular, it is possible to create a unified picture of existing and potentially possible religions, to bring them into a single table, which, in turn, makes it possible to significantly facilitate the choice of religion from the multitude of possible ones. Insufficiently grounded and clearly false religions and groups of religions are becoming more recognizable. So, I present to you new unifying religions.

BIBLEISM

As clearly follows from the above analysis of the sermons and history of the life and death of Jesus Christ, set forth in the Gospels, in no way could he be God Himself. The Trinity postulate clearly cannot be true. Three separate persons cannot be at the same time one person - this is **contrary to common sense**. And the fact that Jesus and God are separate persons is beyond doubt. After all, Jesus talked with God, turned to him with a request – "may this cup pass from me." The doctrine of the Trinity defies rational explanation. Christians in the 1st century did not know anything about the concept of the Trinity; it arose much later. Only in 325, at the First Council of Nicaea, was it decreed that Jesus is God and that God and Jesus are one. A few more decades later, the Holy Spirit was added to them, and the Trinity was formed. This is also written about in modern Wikipedia; everyone can get acquainted: "The Trinitarian dogma (the doctrine of the Trinity) is recognized by the overwhelming majority of Christian confessions. Anti-trinitarian trends were severely persecuted, as a result, their prevalence is low. Famous anti-Trinitarians include Isaac Newton, Miguel Servet, John Locke, John Milton, William Penn, Thomas Jefferson, Henry Longfellow, Joseph Priestley, David Ricardo, Gáspár Bekes, Linus Pauling, and Jerome Salinger. The doctrine, in their opinion, defies rational explanation, because it is not clear how one God can consist of three separate, "unmerged" personalities who can converse with one another. The Trinity is an arbitrary and contradictory distortion of primordial Christianity. Neither in the Old nor in the New Testaments there is neither the term Trinity, nor direct indications of its existence. If Jesus really were equal to God, then it is natural to expect that this fundamental truth would be unequivocally expressed by Jesus or, at least, by one of his disciples, but nowhere in the Gospels does Jesus call himself God, only Christ and the Son of God; there is no identification of Jesus with God in other books of the New Testament. Jesus in the Gospels in clear terms separated himself from God: "About that day, or hour, no one knows, neither the angels of heaven, nor the Son, but only the Father" (Mark 13:32), "Why do you call me good? No one is good but God alone" (Mark 10:18), "My Father is greater than me" (John 14:28) and many others. Christian theologians answer this list of contradictions that the Trinity is a mystery beyond the reach of the limited human mind. But then the question arises whether this limited mind has the right to make specific conclusions about the structure of God, and even more so - to give these statements the status of dogma. Opponents of the Trinity believe that the wording "God is one in three persons" was entrenched in Christianity under the influence of the pagan philosophy of polytheism and under strong political pressure and they view the concept of the Trinity as a distortion of the original Christianity, incompatible with the Gospel definitions: "This is eternal life, may they know You , One True God, and Jesus Christ sent by You" (John 17: 3) and "One God, one mediator between God and men, the man Jesus Christ Jesus" (1 Tim. 2: 5). Leo Tolstoy considered the Christian doctrine of the Trinity confusing, contrary to common sense and the idea of monotheism. In his essay "A Study of Dogmatic Theology," he wrote that the doctrine of the Trinity is "contrary to human reason ... a terrible, blasphemous dogma": "It is impossible to believe that God, my good father (according to the teaching of the church), knowing that salvation or destruction mine depend on the comprehension of Him, the most essential knowledge of myself would be expressed in such a way that my mind, given by Him, cannot understand His expression, and (according to the teaching of the church) would hide all this truth, most necessary for people, under hints ... to the human mind and having no foundation either in Scripture or in Tradition, for me there is still an inexplicable reason that forced the church to confess this senseless dogma and so diligently select fictional proofs of it." As a substantiation of the doctrine of the Trinity, its supporters (Trinitarians) use a synthetic approach, combining separate **indirect** indications from the Old and New Testaments." You can see them right there on Wikipedia. None of them, and even their combination, clearly cannot withstand the clear and precise statements of Jesus Christ, which leave no room for any misinterpretation.

I think Christian leaders should understand that completely, 100%, you cannot be sure that Jesus is God. And if there is even the slightest chance that he is not God, then excessive exaltation of Jesus, turning him into an object of worship, is a violation of the first commandment, a violation of monotheism. And God, having seen the result of the fact that He sent His Envoy to people, will never do it again. So, by and large, it is not in their interests.

The conclusion clearly follows from the above: The most promising of all religions based on faith in God, i.e., the **broadest** of them, capable of uniting the largest number of followers, and, at the same time, **conforming to the truth**, discarding the obviously contradictory options that recognize Jesus as God Himself or His part (part of the Trinity), is a religion that unites **all four possible options** for attitudes towards Jesus Christ: Denying his connection with God (**Judaism**), recognizing him as a man - a prophet of God (**Prophetism**), recognizing him as the Envoy of God (**Envoism**) and recognizing him as the future Messiah, i.e., those who will come and bring radical positive changes to life on Earth (**Messianic Christianity and Messianic Judaism**). I called such a **unifying** religion **Bibleism** (Biblism,

Biblicism, Biblicalism, United Unitarism, General Unitarism, The Religion of the Indivisible God, RIG). **Thus**, a new, potentially possible religion, **Bibleism**, unites **both** the religions created by the Jews, **Judaism and Messianic Judaism, as well as a number of related religions that arose on their basis.** This, in my opinion, is the **widest possible religion for those who believe in God**, allowing to increase the number of adherents while maintaining the foundations. **Bibleism unites everyone who believes in the One and INDIVIDUAL God on the basis of the Torah and the Bible as a whole, regardless of their relationship to Jesus Christ, with the exception of the categorically rejected option that Jesus is God Himself.** This includes, as possible options, all existing types of relationship to Jesus Christ, everything except Jesus - God, rejecting completely only that which is impossible not to reject, against which common sense rebels - the Trinity. After all, the latter option changes not only the attitude towards Jesus, but also the attitude towards God - the possibility of His division into a number of separate persons is recognized. The Bible very clearly, unequivocally states that Jesus is not God Himself. In my opinion, the trends of Christianity that recognize the Trinity can hardly be considered monotheism. **True monotheism is the recognition that God is One and Indivisible**. This is extremely important. The refutation of this fundamental thesis opens the way to idolatry and polytheism, when anyone who has impressed others with the supposedly performed miracles can be declared a god. Also absolutely unreal is the idea that God, albeit Indivisible, left all his affairs, turned into an embryo or a sperm in the body of an earthly woman, became a man Jesus Christ and took terrible torment on the cross (as the Oneness Pentecostals say). So, He was talking to Himself? Thus, in any case, Jesus is not God Himself. One can argue about who he is, what his nature is, but he certainly cannot be God Himself, this is out of the question. And he acted on his own behalf or was associated with God, was at the same time His prophets or the Envoy, and if the Envoy, then whether he will still come as the Messiah to improve the world, we do not know for sure. Bibleism encompasses all these options, emphasizing the need to follow the commandments of God, One and Indivisible. Everything else is not that important. I would also like to note that the monotheism created by the Jews was not just monotheism, but **a combination of monotheism with humanism**. God encourages good and punishes for sins, for immoral behavior - God's requirements **correspond to the requirements of universal human morality**. **Bibleism** accepts for fulfillment the **covenants of the Torah addressed to all people of the Earth**, the covenants of **Injudaism**, as we called them (see above). **At the very least**, of course. For those who consider it necessary to fulfill all the commandments of the Torah or that minimum (225 commandments of the Torah), which corresponds to the concept of Judaism, there may be a religious direction **Bibleism - Judaism** (Judaism - Bibleism). Here is what is very important. If **Jesus is not God, then the question about him is not so fundamental and does not necessarily have to lead to a split into different religions**. And in general, from this point of view, the differences between all these religions and Judaism are not fundamental, since the basis is common (part or all of the commandments of the Torah), and the options for attitudes towards the role of Jesus are accepted precisely as **possible options, not postulates**. In the first century, with the emergence of the Christian community, Judaism included all of these options. But there are also strong arguments against this approach. Just a prophet is one thing, i.e., a person through whom God communicates information to people. Even the most outstanding prophets, Moses and Abraham, with all due respect to them, did not become idols, it never occurs to anyone to pray to them. It is quite another matter - the Envoy of God and the future Messiah. Recognizing Jesus Christ as such almost inevitably turns him into an idol, i.e., actually violating strict monotheism. Therefore, it is necessary to emphasize especially: **Bibleism** does not deny the possibility that Jesus was the Envoy of

God and that he could come as the Messiah, but in Bibleism Jesus is **by no means an idol, an object of worship**, and strict monotheism and the Ten Commandments are not violated. There may also be a narrower version of Bibleism, **Prophet - Bibleism**, combining the options Jesus is the prophet of God, Jesus is the Envoy of God and Jesus is the future Messiah, i.e., cutting off traditional Judaism, which does not recognize the connection of Jesus with God, and in principle there may even be an **Invoy - Bibleism**, cutting off both Judaism and Prophetism.

NEWARISM

A new unifying religion is also possible **Newarism** (Truarism, New Religion, New Uniting Religion, New United Religion, Nurism, Nuarism, Trivarism, Three-Variant Religion), not excluding, along with other possible options (not associated with God or a prophet of God) that Jesus could be the Envoy of the Most High, **but not the future Messiah**. I have already spoken about the reasons for this. According to this new potentially possible religion, it is unlikely that Jesus can be sent to the Jews, whose name is associated with centuries of persecution and murder of Jews, perhaps God has someone to send besides him. In general, nowhere is it said that Jesus is **the only** Son of God, this very concept, "Son of God," is not disclosed in any way. To call Jesus the Messiah only for the alleged removal of original sin from people, while after his arrival nothing, no changes, indicating that he was removed, did not happen, is just stupid. Therefore, **Newarism unites, as possible options, Judaism, Prophetism and Envoism**, excluding the option Jesus - the Messiah or the future Messiah. Everything said about Bibleism applies to Newarism as well. **Newarism** accepts for fulfillment **the precepts of the Torah addressed to all people of the Earth**, the precepts of **Injudaism**, as we called them. **At the very least**, of course. For those who consider it necessary to fulfill all the commandments of the Torah or the minimum that corresponds to the concept of Judaism, there may be a religious direction **Newarism - Judaism**. Jesus in Newarism is by no means an idol, an object of worship, and thus strict monotheism and the Ten Commandments are not violated. There may also be a narrower version of Newarism, **Prophet - Newarism**, combining the options Jesus is the prophet of God and Jesus is the Envoy of God, i.e., cutting off traditional Judaism.

It is impossible to completely exclude the complex **non-equilibrium** religion of **Newarism - Bibleism**. Its main options are options united by **Newarism**, but the option that Jesus will become the future Messiah is not categorically excluded.

NEW JUDAISM

A new "unifying" religion **New Judaism** (New Injudaism, Nujudaism, Nujudism, General Injudaism, Mosheism, Moseism, Moavism, Nuism, Bivarism, Two-Variant Religion), uniting, at least, Injudaism and Prophetism (Injudaism and Prophetism are accepted here as possible options). It differs from Judaism in being **democratic in choosing whether to consider Jesus Christ one of the prophets or not** and whether to fulfill all the commandments of the Torah or at least 200 main ones, common to all, i.e., for Jews and non-Jews, the commandments of the Torah (see below), - it all depends on personal choice. The New Judaism also differs from Judaism in that it may not be related to nationality and is an ordinary missionary religion. Unites all those who believe in a Single and **Indivisible** God who transmits information to people through **people - prophets,** based on the Torah and the Bible as a whole. If we assume that for Judaism it is necessary to fulfill all or at least the 225 commandments of the Torah mentioned above, then the New Judaism is not actually Judaism, and the most correct name for it would be - the New Injudaism. But there can also be **General Judaism** (United Judaism, Broad-Judaism, Common Judaism, United Judaism), which, like Judaism, considers it necessary to fulfill **all the covenants of God** given in the Torah, or at least the 225 main commandments of a Jewish Law. Such as the unification of Judaism with Prophet Judaism as a possible option. Even Christian theologians admit, albeit referring to Jesus: "Jesus said: "You shall love the Lord your God with all your heart" (Matthew 22-37). How does he define the concept of love for God? Answer: "If you love Me, keep My commandments" (John 14-15). **New Judaism and all religions covered by it (Judaism, Injudaism, General Judaism, Prophet-Judaism and Prophetism) believe that information from God to people is transmitted exclusively through people - the prophets. They do not believe that Jesus was one of God's Companions in the Kingdom of Heaven and was introduced into the body of an earthly woman. How? By turning it into a sperm? Or directly into the embryo? Why these difficulties, when it is possible to use people - prophets, giving them, if necessary, the necessary qualities, strengths, abilities, as it was before with other prophets.** It is also possible that a special "divine" material was used to create Jesus. But not a Companion of God. In short, **New Judaism** consists in faith in **the One and Indivisible Creator God, who in the Torah and the Bible as a whole gave us the Law** to fulfill and transmits information to people **through people-prophets**. Such religions are Judaism and the broader **New Judaism with all the religions it embraces**. The differences between them are not fundamental, the choice is yours. Apparently, Jesus was chosen to give Judaism a missionary orientation and thereby ensure its rapid spread around the planet, but perhaps also to give rise to its new direction of the type of religions - **General Judaism, New Judaism or Injudaism**, in which the obligatory connection between religion and nationality (for non-Jews) and mandatory adherence to absolutely all the precepts of the Lord recorded in the Torah is removed. And, perhaps, the right way is to fulfill those requirements set forth in the Torah that apply to all people, and not only to Jews, as proposed by the New Judaism and Injudaism. Although it is clear that this is only the bare minimum. At the same time, those who wish to strictly observe all the covenants of the Lord, obviously, thereby increasing their chances of reward, salvation (afterlife), and entering a Jewish family can also do this by adopting traditional Judaism or, perhaps, if appropriate laws are created, General Judaism.

Considering that it is **the New Judaism and the religions covered by it from those religions** that are based on faith in God that have the greatest chance of conforming to the truth. At the same time, **Judaism and Injudaism** deny the connection of Jesus Christ with God, **Prophetism and Prophetic Judaism** consider him a prophet of God, and **New Judaism and General Judaism** unite both, i.e., all those who believe in the transmission of information from God through people - prophets and, accordingly, that Jesus **may** have been a prophet of God.

New Judaism, as well as Injudaism and Prophetism (in contrast to, respectively, **General Judaism, Judaism and Prophet-Judaism**), honors the **currently valid commandments of the Torah** and, accordingly, the **Bible** as a whole, which apply to all people, not just Jews, and not to the clergy who already know them. That is, every follower of the **New Judaism, Injudaism** or **Prophetism** (and any other religions based on the Torah and the Bible) is free to choose whether to fulfill all the commandments of the Torah or only those listed below. Here are the commandments that must be fulfilled:

Thus, **Injudaism** reduces the number of obligations to observe God's commandments; General Judaism expands the possibilities of a different attitude to Jesus Christ to two options, and **New Judaism** does both, thereby significantly expanding the circle of possible followers with the immutability of the main foundations. Therefore, **it creates the opportunity to follow religions that actually coincide with Judaism, without converting to Jewishness by nationality.**

The **New Judaism** does not contradict either the foundations of Judaism or the foundations of Christianity laid down by the Gospels. It clearly and logically explains what the purpose of Jesus' life and death could be if he really was a prophet of God. After all, if it is impossible to be saved by baptism, if the "original sin" is not removed and the punishment of God has not changed, then it turns out that the torments and death of Jesus were in vain. However, it is quite clear that this is not so, that Jesus did not suffer in vain if the Lord God entrusted him with a special mission - **to bring faith in One God to all the peoples of the Earth**. New Judaism is a religion that combines Strict Judaism, which does not allow the "divisibility" of God, with the main thing in the Torah and the Bible as a whole, except for the doubtful belief in the immaculate conception and, accordingly, that Jesus is not just a possible prophet, but a Envoy from God's Kingdom.

I want to repeat it again. Even though **Bibleism** and **Newarism** are the broadest and most promising religions based on the Torah and the Bible in the sense of the number of possible believers, which **does not contain clearly impossible things**, the possibility that Jesus was one of God's Companions in the Kingdom of God and was introduced into the body of an earthly woman, raises great doubts and healthy skepticism. As I already wrote, it turns out that God turned his close companion, assistant (according to some sources, it was the Archangel Michael) into an embryo or a sperm and placed in the body of an earthly woman. And he also made him go through terrible agony before dying on the cross. Why these difficulties, when you can use people - prophets, giving them, if necessary, the necessary qualities, strengths, abilities, as it was before with other prophets? This turns our gaze to **New Judaism and all religions it embraces (Judaism, Injudaism, General Judaism, Prophet-Judaism and Prophetism)**, which believe that information from God to people is transmitted exclusively through **people - prophets**. Therefore, **New Judaism** and the above religions covered by it are religions **based on the Torah and the Bible, believing in the One and Indivisible God - the Creator and believing**

that information from God to people is transmitted exclusively through people - prophets, and that Jesus Christ is, **possibly**, a prophet of God.

What are the grounds for considering Jesus a prophet of God, despite the presence of statements that, it would seem, could not have been prompted to him by God and which cause, to put it mildly, doubts that he is a prophet or Envoy of God (for example that there is an **eternal** punishment in hell, that you do not need to wash your hands before eating, his unreasonable attacks on supporters of the directions of Judaism that do not recognize it ("scribes"), accusing them of hypocrisy and non-fulfillment of God's covenants). **Such grounds exist**. They are based on the fact that Jesus **left no records,** and we are forced to judge his teaching only from the Gospels. But at that time there was a constant struggle between the existing directions of Judaism among themselves for influence on the minds of fellow citizens. And in this struggle, distortions, hyperboles, and exaggerations were inevitable, caused by the desire to raise the status of Jesus and, accordingly, the prestige of his religious direction, in this case, the original Christianity. Therefore, in the heat of the competition, Jesus could be slandered, at least his words could be distorted, and something could be attributed to him. But there are the most important things that could hardly have been largely distorted, which are repeated in all the Gospels. This **reduction in the requirements for the Sabbath and the doctrine of the existence of an afterlife**, which is repeated many times in various combinations and is the essence of his teaching. Thus, both the denial of the connection between Jesus and God and the recognition of him as a prophet have approximately equal grounds and confirm that the New Judaism that unites them is right in any case and has every right to exist. It is he who is completely free from all those directions that contain things that are in doubt. Therefore, it most closely matches the truth.

Complex non-equilibrium religions **New Judaism - Newarism and New Judaism - Bibleism**, in which the version of **New Judaism** is considered true, are not excluded, but the variants, respectively, **Newarism and Bibleism** are also **completely, categorically not excluded**.

About **General Judaism** (United Judaism). Since it differs from traditional Judaism only by the assumption of the possibility that Jesus could be a prophet of God (as an option) and recognizes the need to fulfill all the commandments of the Torah, or at least the minimum that is necessary for Jews, then the adoption of General Judaism (after passing conversion, of course) may be enough for a person to be recognized as a Jew. At least those people who are **half Jewish by birth**, but not maternal or not entirely maternal. Currently, such people are not recognized as Jews, although for anti-Semites they are Jews and can be persecuted, beaten, pogromed and killed as Jews. By the way, when the blood of different nationalities is mixed, people's abilities do not diminish, but, on the contrary, increase. Therefore, the Jewish genotype developed over centuries of suffering and struggle for survival and the increased abilities of many Jews in the "halves" are not lost, but, in most cases, are intensified.

On the theory of complement, which is adhered to by many prominent representatives of Judaism. According to her, Christianity, including Messianic Christianity and its other forms, is a subsidiary religion of Judaism. These are complementary religions: Judaism is for Jews and those who converted to Judaism and thus became a Jew, Christianity is for non-Jews. And what separates them, **the dogma about Jesus as the Envoy of God and the future Messiah**, may have been necessary at a certain stage to increase the impact on people and faster, as a result, the spread of the Messianic monotheistic Christian religion, but **over time it must necessarily be refuted in the eyes of people**. In this case, Jesus is a prophet, his words were dictated by God. Although it is obvious that much was distorted by his followers, that Jesus was slandered by them. But, as you can see, the recognition of Jesus as a prophet does not entail an accusation of abandoning Judaism. A follower of Judaism is entitled to this point of view. Passed conversion - you are a Judaist. Therefore, the division of Judaism into Judaism proper, General Judaism, Injudaism and New Judaism, possibly with the inclusion of Prophet-Judaism and Prophetism, is conditional. In fact, this is all Judaism. To the greatest extent, it corresponds to what I called Judaism, but does not exclude, at least, **General Judaism and Injudaism**, and **New Judaism**, and in principle, all the directions listed above. It does not require the obligatory complete denial of the possibility of the connection of Jesus, so dear to millions, with God. At least for the followers of some of his directions. And it does not oblige to fulfill absolutely all the commandments. **The creation of such directions as Injudaism, New Judaism, Prophet-Judaism and Prophetism, allows you to become a Judaist without the obligation to be a Jew by nationality, if for some reason you do not want this** - for them the connection between Judaism and nationality is not obligatory. All this allows us to hope that common sense will prevail, and the majority of believers will sooner or later turn to **Judaism** or to one of these very close and in the main directions coinciding with it.

As I already wrote, since the number of commandments performed is a personal matter, in principle, three pairs of religions **Judaism-Injudaism, New Judaism - General Judaism and Prophet-Judaism - Prophetism** can be called, respectively, **Judaism, New Judaism and Prophetism**, considering that such both options are covered by each of these titles.

A few words about modern Christianity. Recently, much has changed for the better in the attitude of Christians towards Jews in comparison with previous centuries. Most branches of Christianity have suspended missionary activity among Jews, recognizing the right of Jews to a "special

Jewish path." In 1965, the Second Council of the Vatican, convened by Pope John XXIII, decreed: "What was done ... cannot be attributed to all the Jews of that time ... Therefore, we must all be careful not to preach ... which is at odds with the gospel and spirit of Jesus." This declaration was reaffirmed by Pope John Paul II: "Hereditary or collective blame cannot be placed on the Jewish people of that time, nor on those who came after them, nor on those who live today." A powerful movement of Christians supporting Jews, Zionism (a movement for gathering Jews who want to live in the Holy Land of their ancestors), the State of Israel, its right to the land of Palestine bequeathed to the Jews by God and recognizing that the Jews "are by nature the people of God..." and "... sanctified by Him" (Dogmas of the Church, 11, 2, p.287). Some of the Christian movements (Evangelical Christians) are even more radical in their attitude towards the Middle East conflict than the majority of Jews themselves, considering it necessary to return all disputed territories to the Jews completely and officially, i.e., all the lands of today's Palestine and the Golan Heights - in fulfillment of the commandment of the Almighty, as well as the undeservedly forgotten decision of the League of Nations in 1922. Unfortunately, anti-Semitism in the world is still very widespread and even gaining strength, while religion is losing its positions. Perhaps the emergence of such religions as New Judaism, Bibleism, Prophetism will breathe new strength into it and stop the moral decline of society.

No matter how you relate to the idea of God, the significance of what happened in history, when the Torah and the Ten Commandments were given to mankind through the Jews, can hardly be overestimated. In a world practically without morality, without a moral law, in which only the right of the strong reigned in its pure form, a moral law was introduced, which for many subsequent centuries significantly softened and improved the climate of relations between people in the world. It is absolutely clear that in the absence of such a law in general, the moral progress of mankind would have been much more difficult. In general, the importance of humanistic religions for humanity can hardly be overestimated. Only two things in the world contribute to a person being a Human in the highest sense of the word, so that he, at least, is not a vile egoist, does not cause harm to another - this is the **correct upbringing** (including books and other media) and humanistic religion. From this point of view, **all humanistic religions** are useful. But I want religion to have a chance to correspond to the truth, without unnecessary fantasies. I hope, dear readers, that this book will help you in this choice. I would also like to say about the inadmissibility of diktat, including the diktat of religion in matters of everyday life of people and, accordingly, pressure on religion from non-believers and the authorities.

Those who believe in God should understand: The preservation of the Jews for so many centuries as a people, despite life among other nations and all the persecutions, and **the revival of the Jewish state**, is a miracle given by the Almighty, and **a good sign** for all peoples of the Earth. This means that the soil is being prepared; it means that **the Messiah is coming**, which should be a Jew from the tribe of King David, a man, a prophet through whom God can change our world for the better. Therefore, everything possible must be done to ensure the security of Israel. **Israel must live! Otherwise, the Messiah may never come.**

UPHISM

First about agnosticism. **Agnosticism** can be different. Some of the supporters of almost any of the religions are actually agnostics, and not true believers. These agnostics are almost believers who generally consider themselves believers, but doubt, are not completely sure of their faith. As a rule, they still try to comply with the basic requirements of religion and, accordingly, morality. But there are other agnostics, who are practically non-believers, although they position themselves as agnostics and sometimes declare a breadth of views, openness to any possibilities. As a rule, these are people who have not chosen one of the existing religions for themselves, who doubt them, or who do not think seriously about these issues. Most often, they are atheists who only declare their openness to any variants of philosophical views. Therefore, their level of moral obligations is much lower and practically does not depend on their beliefs, but is determined by upbringing and spiritual qualities, as with all atheists who are not dominated by the fear of "sin." Moreover, as a rule, they do not consider effective and necessary prayers, including joint ones, although they sometimes resort to them in difficult circumstances. Personally, I would very much like there to be such an **agnostic** community, a teaching whose participants and followers, regardless of whether one or another of them chose a particular religion as the closest to their views or not, would consider it necessary **to live in accordance with the requirements of high**

moral standards. And indeed, logic tells us that if for some reason there is a punishment for violations of moral norms, then we should behave accordingly. Then it will be a working, effective agnosticism, covering all possible options and, accordingly, religions. Such a community, such a movement, a teaching, I called it "**Uphism**" (according to the first letters of the English words "United Philosophy" – "United Philosophy," a Common Philosophy), could, perhaps, eventually unite all people, eliminating the division into different religions and philosophies, competing and sometimes hostile to each other. The motto of this teaching is: We do not know who is right, but we do everything that is necessary based on any existing assumptions. **If there is a punishment, we do everything to prolong our days on Earth and make us happy, so that we get sick less and live longer, and, if there really is such a possibility, so that death does not mean the end for us. If there is no punishment, then at least we get pleasure from the consciousness that we live according to the laws of morality and our conscience is calm**. Uphism believes that, most likely, one way or another, **we will be punished for our sins**. There may also be **Agnosticism - Uphism**, for those agnostics who believe that if we do not deny the possibility of punishment for sins, then we should live observing moral norms. Thus, the new unifying philosophy of **Uphism** is distinguished by the understanding that if we **do not deny the possibility of punishment for sins**, which is common to almost all religions, if we do not exclude such an option as a real one, **then we must live observing the moral norms** that coincide with the basic requirements of the overwhelming majority of religions. It is considered very likely that a person's future (after death or in this world) depends on how he lives. Unlike **Agnosticism - Uphism**, it unites **everyone who thinks so, including followers of various religions**. Uphism is possible as a philosophy - F-Uphism, and as a philosophical and religious movement - D-Uphism. The latter emphasizes the importance of prayer, especially joint prayers, organizes them, being in the ritual sense a religion.

This is a unifying philosophy associated with Uarism (United Religion) or Punishism or with one of its types. So, as in Uarism-Punishism, many types of Uphism are possible. It's just that Uphism is a union of Uphism with the most common religion, **Uarism**, which speaks of punishment for sins (i.e., for violations of the laws of morality) and embraces all religions. Uphism could also play the role of a **single religion, a single faith** for all the inhabitants of the Earth, **uniting** adherents of all religions and modern agnostics, i.e., it could become a religion in the ritual sense, uniting those who consider it necessary to pray together and, possibly, other traditional religious rituals. I consider myself a Uphist, an Agnostic-Uphist. I am sure that a person has the right to doubt and should not be punished for it - if he does not violate the laws of morality. Just as in every religion there are people who seem to be its followers, but in fact, to one degree or another doubt the postulates of the religion they consider themselves followers of, but because of this they do not cease to be considered its followers, so the followers of **Uphism** can consider themselves at the same time followers of the broadest religion - **Uarism as a single religion covering all existing humanistic religions** (see below).

KARMAISM

Now **about religion**.

It is established that in addition to consciousness, directly controlled by the brain, there is also a subconscious component in us. It does not in practice does not depend on consciousness. Scientists know about this. Apparently, it depends, at least to a large extent, on the reaction of the organism as a whole.

Here's an example. The TV show showed a man who lost his memory many years ago after a strong blow. He tried to restore his memory at an institute dealing with the problems of the brain and subconsciousness. Gradually, his memory returned to him. Scientists somehow connected with his subconscious, learned facts from his life, told him, and he gradually remembered them too, and the accompanying facts too. Suddenly, he interrupted the memory recovery process and refused to continue it further. It turned out that he remembered something criminal (some kind of crime he had committed) and was afraid that the subconscious mind would reveal it. Thus, the subconscious mind does not depend on the mind controlled by the brain. This is what I know. I am sure that scientists know many similar examples and more deeply.

To make it clearer that the subconscious mind does not depend on consciousness but depends on the reaction of the organism as a whole, which has a "different" consciousness, I will give data on trees and plants in which there is no brain as such. Experiments carried out by biologists show that plants can see, taste, touch and hear. They can suffer, feel fear, communicate with each other, perceive hatred and love, remember, and think. In short, they have consciousness and feelings.

From the article "Feelings of Plants": "When we counted the annual rings on trees cut down in Russia, we saw that they had some kind of flawed rings, not so wide and even and with an unhealthy color, and all the trees showed a "disease"- 5 -6 such defective rings in a row, falling on 1941-1945. It turns out that the trees felt that something terrible was happening and suffered along with the people. The lie detector sensors were attached to the window flower. When they began to cook lunch nearby and the shrimp were dipped into boiling water through pauses, each time the recorder displayed a sharp peak. When a man next to him cut himself and burned the wound with iodine, the recorder immediately jerked and began to move. One man tended a flower. Another did harm to the flower: he broke branches, pricked leaves with a needle, burned them with fire. As soon as the "villain" entered the room, the recorder began to draw sharp peaks. If the "benefactor" entered, the peaks were replaced by a straight line, the alarm went away. On one side of the sprout, two leaves were pierced, then they were removed so that nothing would remind of them, and then, despite this, all the new branches, leaves, buds of the flower turned out to be on its side opposite to the one from which the injections were made. In the greenhouse, devices were installed that noted, when the soil dried out, that the bean shoots that grew there began to emit low-frequency pulses. As soon as the devices perceived such a signal, a special device immediately turned-on watering. The plants have developed a conditioned reflex. As soon as they needed watering, they immediately gave a signal. A large walnut tree was beaten with a stick. Analyzes have shown that in its foliage during the "execution" in a matter of minutes the percentage of the substance tannin, which has a detrimental effect on pests, has sharply increased. And its leaves become inedible for animals. Once a ficus "fell in love" with a girl. As soon as she entered, the flower experienced a surge of emotions - on the monitors it looked like a sinusoid of bright red color. Once the girl allowed herself to flirt with a colleague, and the ficus began ... to be jealous. Yes, with such force that the instruments were off scale. And the solid black stripe on the monitor indicated which black pit of despair the plant had plunged into. The tree is able to distinguish the psi-fields of individual people, to remember those who harmed them, and to strike back at its enemy with a clot of its field, which can lead to disease.

So, plants have consciousness, although they do not have a brain. Obviously, the same consciousness exists in the human body, along with the consciousness that the brain controls. And this second consciousness, the subconscious, as we say, or some part of it, also reacts to all feelings and to all actions of a person. It knows everything, you can't hide from it. It feels the pain of another and understands when he himself is the source of this pain. And it judges its carrier, reacting painfully to what it perceives as evil. If we, seeking some benefits in dishonest ways, hurting others, with the help of the brain can extinguish impulses of conscience, then our subconscious mind cannot. The result is discomfort and, as a result, illness of varying severity, and sometimes death. Unfortunately, we, as a rule, do not notice this connection. Obviously, our life is so dynamic and changeable in comparison with existence in a plant that our subconscious mind lags far behind the events taking place in reaction speed, and for us, for our brain, any connection between "crime and punishment" becomes elusive. Most likely, it is carried out according to the totality of several human actions, in accordance with his "karma." This is at the moment the main explanation of the new religion based on the disclosure of the indicated connection. I call this religion **Karmaism**. I am sure that this correctness is confirmed by statistics that the average life expectancy of criminals is significantly less than the average life expectancy of people in general. Although, perhaps, the mechanism of the subconscious is different. But it is almost certain that the subconscious mind exists and affects us and our health. **By doing bad things to others, we also hurt ourselves**. Although there is no hard evidence yet, I think this assumption cannot be attributed to pure faith, rather, it is a scientific hypothesis, and I believe that sooner or later it will be proven.

The existence of thinking in our country, independent of the brain, is also evidenced by the data on the possibility of thinking without a brain in a living person. From the article "Is it possible to think without a brain?" on the site mk.ru: Let's turn to the research of Professor John Lorber of the University of Sheffield. One of Sheffield's students had a good academic record and had an IQ of 126. However, after scanning, Lorber found that his patient's brain was almost completely absent. In his skull was found only a layer of cerebral tissue less than 1 millimeter thick, covering the upper end of the vertebral nerve. The rest of the space was filled with water. The student suffered from impaired circulation of cerebrospinal fluid, in which it accumulates in the cranium. This student was able to live a normal life and even graduate with honors from the university. In 1970, a New Yorker passed away at the age of 35. He worked as a concierge and did a good job of routine tasks: keeping an eye on the steam boiler. The autopsy revealed almost complete absence of the brain. Professor Lorbera identified several hundred people who were quite mentally developed, despite a very small number of brain cells, some of them had an almost complete absence of a brain. There are also examples when people received severe brain injuries and continued to live without a significant part of the brain matter, remaining a capable person. For many years there has been a struggle in this area between two concepts. The first point of view assumes that consciousness, thinking, and memory are nothing more than the result of the functioning of the brain itself. The second of them goes back to the idea of the existence of a non-biological agent, a carrier of consciousness, thinking and individuality of a person. According to these ideas, the brain plays only the role of an intermediary between the intelligent "I" and the physical body, organizing and ordering human activities. And physical death by no means presupposes the cessation of the existence of the consciousness of the individual and his attributes. On the contrary, the survival of the conscious "I" belonging to a more subtle level, primary in comparison with gross matter, becomes quite logical and appropriate. In the field of science called parapsychology, a huge amount of evidence has been accumulated confirming the validity of this concept. Among them are the phenomena of mediumship, out-of-body experience - both during clinical death and induced by special methods, the ability of consciousness to receive information about objects remote in space and time, and much more. According to the world-famous neurophysiologist, Nobel Prize winner John Eccles, in addition to the material world, there is a world of ideas. Human thinking appears because of the interaction of two worlds in the brain, the world of ideas influences the functioning of the brain by changing the probability of the release of mediators in synaptic contacts. Professor Wilder Penfield, in his book The Mystery of the Mind, proves that the mind is completely independent of the brain: "It is an absolutely independent entity. The mind commands, the brain executes." We are not just our body.

This second option also implies another version of the explanation of punishment already during life, let's call it **Soul - Karmaism** - this is **the existence of the soul**, i.e., that lump of energy and matter that remains to live after the death of a person. For those who believe in the soul, it is quite clear that it is independent of the brain, because it exists when the brain is no longer there. The soul both reacts to our behavior and punishes us for sins.

So, I present to you the new religion of Karmaism, in the truth of which I am almost convinced. **Karmaism is the belief that a person's future depends on how he lives** (on his "karma"), and **the punishment for sins, i.e., for violations of the laws of morality, occurs already during this life**, i.e., our future does not depend on external rational forces - this is the law of nature. Punishment for sins already during this life is not obvious, because it usually comes much later than "sins," so late that we cannot grasp the connection between them, but it is - a person who does not follow the laws of morality begins to get sick and rather dies. Those **sins are one of the causes of illness and death** - most likely, not the only one, natural causes have not been canceled either. In this case, **it is incorrect to make a comparison between people, this is all very individual**, - often this person could live longer or be healthier if he was better, did not violate the norms of morality. There are certain arguments in favor of this, associated with the properties of water, of which we are more than 70% composed, with a change in its structure in the case of bad human behavior, i.e., most likely, the **subconscious** is acting here, or some then other mechanisms that are not associated with external intelligent forces (except, possibly, the influence of other people, their anger and envy). And the punishment, I am sure, does not depend on the axioms, not on what we believe in, but on how we live. You can avoid just punishment under the law, but you cannot run away from yourself, from your own uncontrollable court. I think the bare minimum is as follows: **Don't kill; don't torture, don't maul; don't rape; don't take away; don't steal; don't perjury; don't slander; don't cheat (both in your personal life and to your people); honor your parents; take care of children.** A variant of this religion, **Karmaism-Futurism**, is also possible, combining belief in punishment for sins already during this lifetime with belief in an afterlife, but without any further punishment. And then it becomes clear (in contrast to Futurism), due to what forces this punishment is carried out. **Futurism** here means a group of religions that believe in an afterlife even without the existence of God - existing **Buddhism, Soul - Buddhism**, Scientology and new, potentially possible, **New Buddhism and Langs** (see below).

I would also like to give evidence that even many prominent representatives of Christianity believe that punishment overtakes us already in this life, and not only necessarily in the next world, not to mention the followers of Judaism, who every Yom Kippur await the decision of their fate Almighty for the next year (entries in the Book of Life). Here is what Yuri Lutsenko writes: "Somewhere a misconduct is registered and after a while it returns as an event in our destiny. Therefore, many are unaware of why they have such a difficult fate. Let's say a person is hurt. If we consider justice not in the context of 'here and now,' but in the context of the whole past life, where a person has repeatedly sinned, it is necessary to comprehend what happened through the prism of the well-known phrase 'what you sow, you reap a hundredfold.' It is this justice that rules the world. For a crime - an inevitable punishment. The absence of resentment is sincere forgiveness through a logical awareness of responsibility for each of your actions. The offended person views the offender as a mediator of the Law in the return of sin and recognizes the right to punish himself for wrongdoing. The sinner is clean in this episode before the Law. He redeemed it by suffering. Let me give you the anatomy of stress and the onset of illness in the physical body. We consist of cells, they, in turn, of molecules, atoms and further protons, neutrons, electrons. Impulses of resentment, fear, jealousy, envy cause the 'confusion' of the atom, i.e., violation of the normal interaction of elementary particles, cells, biochemical processes in the body. The first phase of the disease begins. With the continuous pressure of a mass of negative emotions, the disease becomes more severe. It is impossible to get rid of the negativity that destroys our life without a correct worldview, which contains the knowledge of the Laws of the life of this world."

There is one more possible explanation of the phenomenon of punishment during this life, i.e., religion **Karmaism**, of course, is fantastic, but the reality of which also cannot be completely excluded. Let's call this variant **Field Karmaism**. It follows logically from the shortcomings of Darwin's theory of natural selection. If intraspecific changes due to heredity and variability quite satisfactorily explain the process of evolution, then the creation of more no less perfect new forms by blind nature seems to be an absolute miracle. After all, if nature is blind and progress is a simple enumeration of options, then some unsuccessful transitional forms must have existed. However, these are not observed. All species and their individual organs always appear already in a form, quite ready for "use." There are three possible ways out to explain this. Two are known: either there is a certain Higher Mind, God, i.e., evolutionary progress is carried out not by blind nature, but by God, about whose nature we know absolutely nothing, or there is some natural method about which we still know nothing. I would like to suggest another possible option. It is possible that **nature is not blind, but has a certain level of intelligence and, of course, feelings**. That is, not only individual representatives of nature - animals, plants - but also **earthly nature is a kind of sensory-intellectual (sensory-informational) field**. Until the organ is ready, nature, i.e., the specified field feels like it shouldn't be used. And it not only contributes to the creation of new forms, organs, etc., ready for life, but also reacts negatively to all kinds of bad deeds that violate a certain positive balance in nature and **punishes us** for violations of moral norms. It is possible, at the same time, that when we feel very bad, especially for many people at the same time, it feels and reacts with hurricanes, earthquakes, volcanic eruptions, etc. That is, the earth as a whole, or at least its surface layer, in which we and all other living organisms are located, is able to react to the feelings of people, which sometimes manifests itself in natural disasters and in a negative impact on the health of those who deserve punishment, and also, perhaps in some kind of assistance to certain people or their communities by providing a certain beneficial effect. This is a special field, I think, rather sensory, sensory-biological than intellectual, but, of course, with a certain intellectual component, i.e., with varying degrees of intelligence. This field is, so to speak, our God, although in an intellectual sense it is probably weaker than us. But it is precisely this that can punish us for sins, and sometimes catch our desires and help us.

UNITED RELIGION (UARISM)
AND PUNISHISM

The religion **Uarism** or **United Religion**, is **the belief in punishment for sins, in the fact that the future of a person, and not necessarily only in the afterlife, but, perhaps, already during this life, depends on how he lives.** Some forces exist that affect us, although we do not know their nature, whether they are reasonable (One God, with or without helpers, or someone else or something) or not, perhaps it is our own subconscious. This is **an absolute belief in the punishment for sins, that is, for violations of the laws of morality.** The belief that the **future of a person, and not at all necessarily only in the afterlife, which is in question, and possibly already during this life, depends on how he lives.** This is what **all humanistic religions** have in common. If not all are united, but only parts of religions, such a religion is called **Punishism.** It can be connected with one or another more specific religion as the most probable, including (and, I think, in the first place) with any of the unifying religions. Many options are possible depending on which religions are combined. I tried to unite those religions that, in my opinion, can, in principle, correspond to the truth. **The religion uniting Punishism and Futurism, I called simply Punishism.** In other cases, the name will include the religion with which Punishism is connected: **Punishism - New Judaism, Punishism - Prophetism, Punishism - Newarism, Punishism - Bibleism,** etc. In fact, all connections with Punishism with each of the religions based on faith in God encompass **Prolongism**, uniting Futurism with the corresponding religion: **Punishism - Prolongism - New Judaism, Punishism - Prolongism - Prophetism, Punishism - Prolongism - Bibleism**, etc. As I said, if Punishism is not united with any one religion, but unites **all humanistic religions**, I propose to call such a common religion - **Uarism (United Religion). Uarism and all variants of Punishism speak of punishment for sins but leaves open the question of whether it is carried out in this life or in the afterlife and by what forces it is carried out - is it God or our subconscious** (or maybe something else). There are so many things in the world that science is not yet able to explain: the mystery of amazing life coincidences in twins, sometimes located at different "ends" of the Earth and not knowing about each other's existence, the mystery of clairvoyance and other things that speak about the action of some unknown forces. The punishment for violations of moral standards and the possibility of an afterlife are far from the most surprising of them. Followers of **Uarism and Punishism** say: We do not know exactly how the punishment is carried out, already during this life or after death, i.e., in another world or after the soul has entered another being (in another person), and at the expense of what forces. This is not the main thing for us. **We believe that the main thing is not what a person thinks, what his views are, but how he lives. How he behaves.** And we consider the requirements of observance of the laws of morality to be the necessary **requirements for people.** By the way, they practically coincide with the requirements set forth in the laws of the Torah and, accordingly, the Bible as a whole, addressed to all people, and not just to the Jews. **The main tenet of Uarism and Punishism: If you do not violate the gross norms of morality, do not achieve your goals by meanness, slander, fraud, and other dishonest ways, do not harm people, then you will not be punished**. And if you also do good deeds, help, resist, if possible, evil, then perhaps you will be encouraged.

For encouragement, I think, it is necessary to show special altruism up to self-sacrifice, or to fight evil at the risk to your own life or health - usual good behavior is most likely considered the norm. **Uarism and Punishism** with all its variants are based on **Karmaism**, but only as one of the possible variants. All of them are considered absolutely equal and have the same chances of being true. But the variant of **Uarism** is really the only religion that is **common** to all believers, the true **United Religion**. It answers the main question - how should we live in order not to be punished.

     Karmaism, as I already wrote, is only one of the possible options for the religions of **Uarism** and **Punishism**, but it is the main basis for the truth of **Uarism and Punishism**. Or maybe the mechanism of punishment is different, we do not know that. In the end, it doesn't really matter. **The main thing is that there is punishment**, that it awaits everyone who deserves it. This is precisely what **Karmaism, Punishism and Uarism** assert. I am deeply convinced: **Punishment or encouragement of a person does not depend on his thoughts and beliefs, on whether he observes any rituals, but completely depends only on his actions. With good behavior, i.e., if a person does not violate moral standards, he will not be punished**. Surely examples of the truth of this inexhaustible number, they could be cited endlessly. However, the connection between "crime" and punishment is usually not obvious and therefore cannot serve, unfortunately, as a rigorous proof. As I already wrote, by and large, as a person, I am only interested in one thing: How can I live so as not to be punished. Searching for answers to more specific questions is hardly advisable, since causes a split and confrontation between the followers of different concepts, and no one has serious evidence.

Nevertheless, if you have doubts about **Karmaism**, another approach is possible, talking about the punishment for sins. This is the new unifying religion of **Prolongism**. It is based on Futurism, unites all humanistic religions, except for Karmaism and wider Uarism, and speaks of punishment for sins either by God or other forces, but, unlike Karmaism, already in the afterlife. Like Uarism, it can be combined, in addition to Futurism, with one or another religion associated with belief in God: **Prolongism - Bibleism, Prolongism - New Judaism**, etc., excluding several religions that seem to her to be clearly false, from consideration.

So, the above are possible explanations for **Karmaism**. And on it are based **Punishism** and the **United Religion - Uarism**, which talk about **punishment for sins**, but without specifying how and by what forces it is carried out. The creation of these religions and, especially, the **United Religion**, based on values common to **all humanistic religions**, is an important step in overcoming existing strife, hostility between followers of different religions, in **uniting all people on Earth**, as well as in correcting morals through faith in punishment for violations of the laws of morality. This is especially important given the fact that in fact only two things on Earth can contribute to a person's mastery of the principles of high morality - this is the correct **upbringing** (family, art) and the **belief** that you will be punished for bad, immoral behavior. This kind of faith give to a person **Karmaism, Punishism and the United Religion - Uarism**. The choice is yours.

In conclusion, I want to emphasize once again: I am really worried about only two questions - **how to live so as not to be punished** (if punishment exists), and **whether there is life after death** (afterlife), and also whether punishment is already carried out in this life or in the afterlife. As to the questions regarding how and by what forces this can take place, I do not really care. Therefore, for me, the closest religions are the religions of **Uarism (United Religion)**, which corresponds to the truth exactly, if at least one of the existing or potentially possible humanistic religions corresponds to it, and the religion of **Karmaism**, on which it is based. I absolutely do not believe in the Trinity. I repeat once again: **Three persons cannot make up at the same time one single person**. This is contrary to common sense. This also contradicts the words of Jesus, for example: "**Why do you call me good? No one is good but God alone**" (Matthew 10-18). Yes, and the transformation by God of one of his companions into a sperm or an embryo and its introduction into the body of an earthly woman is unlikely. Why such difficulties? For the same purposes, you can use people-prophets, giving them the necessary abilities. If I believed in God, I would be a follower of **New Judaism**. But for me **Judaism, Injudaism and General Judaism** are also possible. Also, **Prophetism, Prophet - Judaism, Newarism** and the most general of the potentially truthful religions, the religion of **Bibleism**, which allows to maximize the number of adherents, are not excluded. And for other people, probably also the religions **Envoism and Messianic Christianity** are not excluded. I emphasize once again: For those who believe in God, New Judaism is the most consistent with the truth. After all, **New Judaism**, which has preserved the essence and spirit of traditional Judaism and, thereby, excludes dubious options, but **does not answer with a categorical "no" to the question of whether Jesus Christ could be a prophet of God**, who enjoys the love of a large number of people all over the world, and to a large extent removed the obstacles to its spread among the peoples due **to the decrease in the number of commandments that must be followed and the removal of ties with the nationality**, has a **real chance** of becoming one of the world's leading religions, uniting hundreds of millions of believers. However, **Bibleism and Newarism** have even more chances, although they contain some provisions that give rise to doubts, but the choice is yours.

What does it mean to live so as not to violate moral standards? It is absolutely clear that the bare minimum here is not to violate the current legislation, even in those cases when you are sure that you will be able to hide the crime you are committing or even a minor offense. Although this depends on the laws of a given country. Often, especially under authoritarian regimes, some of the laws are humiliating towards people, serve the ruling stratum and do not coincide with the requirements of morality. And vice versa. There are many such actions of people who do not formally violate the law, but in fact are vile and unfair. For example, violation of marital fidelity in conditions where divorce is possible, poor care of children, elderly parents, libel and much more. Given that fair competition is perfectly acceptable and normal. The main thing is to be guided by the rule stemming from the Torah and, accordingly, from the Bible as a whole: When the Torah scholar Hillel was asked how to express the essence of the Torah in one sentence, he said: "**Do not do to another what you do not want to be done to you.**" This is the basic rule of morality. No matter how you relate to the idea of God, the wisdom and correctness of the Torah and the Bible hardly raises doubts - it is fully consistent with the laws of morality. If you do not believe in God, you can exclude from them what is related to belief in God. But this does not cancel the requirements necessary for normal human life. And if you break them, then do not be surprised that you will be punished for it.

But apart from ordinary everyday life, in which everything seems to be clear, there is also a more complex and ambiguous thing of politics. There are not many political movements that have clearly and unconditionally discredited themselves in the eyes of the overwhelming majority of the world's inhabitants. There is Fascism, Nazism. Socialism, which inevitably leads to a dictatorship and sometimes to the horrors of mass extermination of people, seemingly also discredited itself, but, oddly enough, has recently been enjoying increasing popularity in Western countries. But there is also a large number of political movements and processes that are undoubtedly harmful to people, but this is absolutely not obvious for many people, moreover, a large number of people support with all their souls and sometimes by all means political movements that are objectively harmful to them or will harm them in future. In this regard, I would like to consider the political situations in the United State of America and in the Israel.

THE UNITED STATES
OF AMERICA

Economic development data show that the most successful economic development and the highest standard of living took place in those states in which Republicans and Democrats replaced each other more often. And in those states in which one of these parties ruled for a long time, and, moreover, almost regardless of whether they are Republicans or Democrats, the results of economic development were the worst. And the reason for this is clear. When representatives of one of these approaches have been in power for too long, pulling the blanket over themselves for too long, this has a bad effect on the economy and, consequently, on the living standards of members of society. This, obviously, manifests the action of the universal law that any extremes are always bad and can ruin any, even the best, idea. Under the long rule of the Democrats, as a rule, the layer of officials unjustifiably grows, "outsourcing" increases, and under the long rule of the Republicans, polarization in incomes increases, gradually reducing the number of people with sufficient purchasing power. Both lead to a decrease in the rate of economic development. The Republican periods are generally more successful, but the overall trend continues. The same pattern is true for the country. In my opinion, **this is the law of the functioning of the market economy - to achieve maximum efficiency, the democratic and republican (labor and conservative) approaches should periodically**

replace each other. Or you need to constantly use both approaches so that in each of the sectors of the economy, thanks to the periodic change in these approaches in it (depending on its state at the moment) and, accordingly, in society as a whole, the necessary balance is maintained between the interests of business and people of hired labor. Long-term use of the same one-sided approach is a terrible thing that can ruin any economy. No matter how much we would like to reduce the degree of property stratification in society, we must not neglect the laws of the market economy, otherwise everyone will suffer. The constant change in power of the Republican and Democratic parties every eight years on average has resulted in unprecedented economic growth and America's transformation into the most successful and prosperous nation in the world. Here is what the writer Mikhail Weller writes: "Man is the spearhead of evolution. And every civilization in the process of social evolution has its own life span, goes through its phase cycles. Our civilization is at its peak, has reached an unprecedented prosperity in history, comfort, level of freedom. And **now the changes are a descent from the top into the abyss**: such is the relief of the historical path. People always build a happy future, but having crossed the top, they destroy the happy past with the same good intentions." Anyone who thinks that it is possible to achieve a better life for the majority by worsening the situation of businessmen, taking away from them what, in his opinion, they have appropriated unfairly, is deeply mistaken. The existing graded scale of taxes takes away a lot from them. Of course, the absence of a tax scale, i.e., levying taxes strictly proportional to income is unfair and cannot but cause indignation of ordinary workers. But the existing graduated scale is cool enough. If you make it even cooler, a decrease in the interest of business owners will only lead to an even greater transfer of businesses abroad and to a slowdown in the pace of economic development, which will affect everyone. Favorable conditions for business are an immutable law of a market economy, and by worsening them, we are acting

PERMAN

not only against the rich, but also against the poor, against all segments of the population. The best conditions for "ordinary" people worsen the conditions for business (which, in turn, negatively affects their well-being, but not so clearly and not to the same extent in the short term), and vice versa. The only way out is to find the "golden mean," the necessary balance of interests. In the United States, it has so far been supported naturally by the occasional change in power between Democrats and Republicans. Neither side encroached on the foundations, did not set itself the task of radically changing the country, what ensured its prosperity. I called this political position, which requires a periodical change of "republican" and "democratic" approaches, the **New Centrism.**

However, a number of changes should have been carried a long time ago. In my opinion, it has long been necessary to put more serious **barriers against illegal immigration**, which threatens with the legalization of illegal immigrants over time, and, in particular, before the penetration of potential terrorists from the most hostile, radicalized and dysfunctional Islamic states into the country. Illegal immigration is inextricably linked to drug trafficking and many other criminal offenses, it reduces the security of residents of the United States.

Another important aspect of the capitalist system that should be strengthened is **anti-monopolistic** policy, the fight against the dominance of monopolies. True capitalism, in short, **is competition**. That is what provides its main advantages. In my opinion, the anti-monopoly legislation is not tough enough, the fight against the dominance of monopolies is not being carried out decisively enough. This is bad for the economy and the economic situation of people. Many monopolists, in pursuit of maximum profits, either pay their workers so little that the state is forced to pay them extra to the official minimum for the family at the expense of taxpayers, or, taking advantage of their monopoly position, they inflate prices. All of

93

this is simple robbery. It must be fought. The goal of **narrowing the gap between rich and poor as much as possible** is also very important. It is simply unacceptable to do this by force, increasing the percentage of tax from the rich. This, as already mentioned, does not work; on the contrary, it leads to a capital flight from the country and to a decrease in the rate of economic development. But it is **necessary to drastically tighten antitrust laws** and **strengthen incentives for charity**, i.e., the tax benefits arising from it.

It has long been necessary to fight **left liberalism** (progressivism). The essence of the current dominant trend in him is that sympathy for the weak is hypertrophied to the point of complete absurdity, to the a priori justification of the weak in everything, including even in those cases when he mocks the strong and kills him, to the actual justification of terror. Everything is allowed for the weak. It promotes what is contrary to the Bible and reduces population growth. Allow children to live in families with two fathers or mothers, although this is likely to traumatize their psyche. Sometimes they sink to such vile, wild things in a civilized society, to such insanity and violation of elementary decency, as shared showers, even shared toilets in educational institutions. They consider themselves forces of Good, fighting against Evil, but at the same time they often use the methods of Evil, believing that only they have the truth, and in the struggle, all means are good, "the end justifies the means." But Good, using the methods of Evil, is Evil, or sooner or later it becomes so.

In connection with the above, it is understandable that the results of the last elections signify a radical turning point in the history of the United States of America, and, possibly, the entire world. They have created the opportunity to fundamentally change the United States for the worse, which threatens it with complete disaster.

Currently, the Democratic Party has both presidential power and a majority in both houses of Congress. In the near future, the Democratic Party, taking advantage of the fact that the president is a Democrat and it also has a majority in both chambers of Congress, in an effort to secure permanent power, can take a number of measures that can **radically change the election situation in its favor without the practical possibility of changing it in the future**. These can be steps such as the legalization of Mexicans and other Latin American illegal immigrants, who mostly vote for Democrats, changing the number of members of the Supreme Court and introducing their supporters into it, and such cardinal constitutional changes as transferring the status of the metropolitan District of Columbia, which always votes for Democrats, to the rank of a state, the same with Puerto Rico, lowering the voting age, etc., and even a complete change in the electoral system. If any of these steps are carried out, it will mean a radical revolution in the United States, meaning the future irremovable power of one party, when only one opinion is true, and all other opinions will be suppressed. **It would be a permanent dictatorship of one Democratic Party**. Currently, this party is largely captured by **left-wing liberals** who are against the traditional family, which ensures the reproduction of the population, **socialists, anti-Semites, Islamists, monopolists,** and those who act in their interests **(globalists), minorities who demand special privileges, those who seek to change the ethnic composition of the country, replacing it with ethnic groups that are now minorities, and those who seek permanent power for their party**. They can be generically called "leftists" or "revolutionaries," because, despite the great differences among themselves, they are united by a common goal - they all want to radically change America, including partially changing its Constitution. These groups have actually seized power in the Democratic Party and, in pursuit of their irremovable power, seek to change history, even sometimes using terrorist organizations and defunding of police forces. Many of them have different, sometimes opposite views. But they have a common goal: they all seek to overthrow, as it seems to them, the "power" of white men, whose works, and talents, basically, created modern America and its main achievements, to make them a minority in the country and, as a result, destroy Great America. Since there are only two leading parties in the United States that have a chance of being in power, it so happened historically that they all concentrated in the Democratic Party, which is more left-wing. Under their pressure and onslaught it has now become a conduit for their main aspirations. Therefore, there can be nothing worse for the development of the economy and democracy in the country than the permanent power of **this** party. This would be a coup, extremely dangerous for America, threatening it not only with a slowdown in economic development and a deterioration in people's living standards, but also with an actual departure from democracy, as well as a possible civil war and complete disintegration into states. And this coup, destructive for the country, has already begun, it is already happening. Programs have been developed to legalize illegal immigrants and transfer the status of the metropolitan District of Columbia to the rank of a state, as well as the "For the People" program, which requires states to automatically register eligible voters in one day, provide citizens with the opportunity to vote 15 days before the election date and receive an absentee ballot without explanation, the ability to vote by mail, as well as the creation of commissions to change the boundaries of electoral districts. That's what one of those whom I call a real Democrat in the ranks of the Democratic Party said (such can still be called Democrats - Conservatives, they are for preserving the values that were laid down by the American Constitution, so they have more in common with Republicans than with the groups listed above, which are in the majority in the Democratic Party, and in principle, their unification with Republicans within the framework of the General Democratic Conservative Party is not excluded), Democratic Senator Joe Manchin, about the Democrats' bill: "This is not the bill, and I do not support it, because it will split us even more. I don't want to live in a divided country. Do we really want to live in America, where one party can dictate and demand everything it wants? I cannot explain strictly one-party electoral reform or the abolition of Senate rules for the sake of one party's agenda. The current debate on how to conduct elections is not aimed at finding common paths, but at gaining an advantage for one party. The Congressional initiative on elections must take into account the interests of both parties, otherwise we risk splitting and destroying our republic, which we, as elected representatives, swore to protect. Our founding fathers had the wisdom to see the temptation of absolute power and build a system of checks and balances to force parties to compromise and preserve democracy." Unlike in the past, the current situation, especially given the recent changes in the Republican Party, unconditionally puts the Republican Party (although it may seem paradoxical to those people who are poorly versed in the current realities) in the position of defender of the entire people, the overwhelming majority of them, against socialists and left liberals (progressives), as well as against the largest monopolies, international corporations and those who support them.

The attack of the left is accompanied by persecution of "dissidents." This is what Nikita Novsky writes in his article "The Liberal Gulag:" "Speaking about the fact that there are intolerant of them, those who assert it themselves become intolerant. All their words about the need to prohibit the right to freedom of thought for those who are intolerant should be applied to them as well. Otherwise, we get the same oppression under the sauce of freedom. The Western world is threatened by an unprecedented wave of violence and intolerance - but not from the right, but from the left, left-liberal side. After all, it is much easier to identify 'heresy' now, and to prove it too, and with the latest tendency of the absence of the presumption of innocence - so in general. And there is no doubt that punishment is planned. The Inquisition is returning in a new, left-liberal guise, and we must stop it."

What is the conclusion from all that has been said? If the Democratic Party manages to change the laws, the Constitution, etc. and to make it so that it becomes permanently ruling, depriving the Republican Party of the chance to come back to power, this will not only mean the actual usurpation of power, but will also lead to the final destruction of democracy and to an economic collapse of an unprecedented scale. The Democratic Party cannot be allowed to do this. It is necessary to explain to people the essence of what is happening everywhere, so that the **Republican Party** will win Congressional and Presidential elections in the next elections. As I already wrote, by the time of the **next elections**, the "Democrats" will make a number of decisions that will significantly reduce the chances of the Republicans to win. But the full package of such measures will not be available yet, and the chances will remain. **This will be the last chance for Republicans and all those who love America! Or in the next two elections (parliamentary and presidential), or never!** Particular attention should be paid to monitoring the integrity and transparency of the voting procedure. Let's not let ourselves be deceived anymore! Everyone who loves America - let's save our country before it's too late!

ISRAEL

As you can see, supporting the Democratic Party in this situation is an absolute sin and sooner or later those who support it will be punished. Most likely, they are digging their own worst future. An even more serious sin is anti-Semitism, hatred of those who belong to the Jewish people, who gave the world faith in the One God. Moreover, Jesus Christ belonged to him, whom the majority of believers consider God Himself, at least His Envoy, His prophet. At the present time, as a rule, he is hiding behind anti-Israelism. In this regard, I consider it necessary to clarify the current situation of Israel, whose actions are absolutely forced, and any state on Earth simply could not behave differently - this is at least, since Israel is under the strongest pressure from the entire world community, fueled by a sense of anti-Semitism, and any other state could afford much more.

What is the essence of the ongoing conflict in Palestine between Arabs and Jews? The current pseudo-peace-loving rhetoric of the leaders of the Arab Palestinian Authority should not deceive anyone. They still have not deleted from their program the demand for the destruction of the Jewish state. This shows that **the essence of the Arab - Israeli conflict is that the Arabs of Palestine do not need their own state next to Israel, their goal is the destruction of Israel**. For their own people, in Arabic, they speak about it directly. Moreover, their power is kept only by the support of Israel. Otherwise, it will immediately be captured by Hamas, a terrorist organization that not only practices explosions, shelling, and murder of the peaceful Jewish population, but also openly declares that its goal is the destruction of Israel. It is precisely on the Hamas side that the sympathies of the absolute majority of the Arabs of the Palestinian Authority, at least 80% of whom, according to all polls, support terror and hate not only Israel, but also the United States and the entire Western world, are on the side of Hamas. Is it really not clear that the creation of another Arab state, unable, as it is already quite clear, to produce anything on its own, except for missiles to bombard Israel, and living on handouts from the world community, cannot reorient the Arabs of Palestine to a peaceful life and promote peace in the Middle East. It will be just another hotbed of hatred and war. Moreover, it is actually located in the very center of Israel and owns the heights dominating over it. If a "Palestinian state" is created, then Israel will no longer be able to control the Samaria heights from which Tel Aviv is being shot. **It will be enough to place artillery installations on the heights of Samaria to turn the lives of the citizens of the center of Israel into a daily hell**. But in the strip under these heights, in the central part of the country, in a very small area, 80% of its inhabitants live, and the arsenal of methods of attack, as the example of Gaza shows, is enormous, and when attempts to resist them, accusations of "exceeding the limits necessary defense." Even if a small and remote from the center of Gaza, voluntarily abandoned by Israel without any conditions, causes such, to put it mildly, troubles, then what will happen when almost all major cities and centers of the country, all of its most densely populated part, are in the immediate vicinity of the terrorists. the capital of the country is Jerusalem with the main state institutions and an airport, which enemies can fire from the heights of Samaria, and the entire territory of Israel underground will be covered with a dense network of tunnels used by terrorists. Little Israel will not be able to continue to exist if its urban infrastructure, airport, and roads are under fire. And it will be almost impossible to defend the country within such borders in the event of war. No wonder they are called the borders of Auschwitz. Martin Sherman: **"Arab control over the heights of Samaria can paralyze the entire country. It would be a constant threat to all the country's most important highways.** Shelling from all types of weapons, bombs, tunnels, etc." Amnon Rubinstein: "Little Israel cannot continue to exist if its urban infrastructure, airport and roads are under fire." And even Shimon Peres wrote in 1978: "If a separate state of the Palestinian Arabs is created, it will be armed from head to toe. There will also be bases of the most radical terrorists, armed with shoulder rockets and threatening not only pass-ers-by, but every plane and helicopter in Israeli airspace and every car moving." Do those who support the Arabs against Israel and shed croco-dile tears of sympathy for the "poor Palestinians" do not understand that they are on the side of the devil, on the side of the most inhuman, inher-ently Nazi forces? Leftist philosophy turns everything upside down, turns the real victim, Israel, into the aggressor, and the Arabs saturated with hatred and thirst for Jewish blood and engaged in terror, who openly declare their plans to destroy Israel and the Jews living in it, into a victim. Why create another Muslim state, which will inevitably become a breeding ground of hatred and terror, and thereby contribute to the death of Israel? After all, **the example of Gaza clearly showed what the consequences would be.** Can there still be some illusions, some doubts after that? Peace with the Palestinian Arabs is impossible for a simple reason - their mini-mum requirements are much larger than the maximum concessions that Israel can make. Former Israeli Prime Minister Golda Meir spoke well of the essence of the conflict and the impossibility of a compromise with the Arabs: **"There is no compromise between Israel's desire to survive and the Palestinian Arabs' desire to destroy it."** Anyone who insists on further territorial concessions to Israel is either an idiot who does not understand their mortal danger to the Jewish state, or its obvious enemy, who wants its destruction. In addition, we must not forget that Israel has all the rights to these lands, i.e. **Judea and Samaria (and Gaza and the Golan Heights too), legally must belong to Israel - and by right of the victor over the aggressor** (like, for example, the Kaliningrad region of Russia and Pomerania and Silesia - the western lands of Poland), **and according to the decision of the League of Nations of July 24, 1922 and, accordingly, in accordance with paragraph 6 and article 80 of Chapter XII of the UN Charter, which oblige to maintain in force and implement this decision, like all decisions of the League of Nations, and from a religious point of view, according to the clearly expressed will of God. In addition, at that time, there was no recognized sovereignty over Judea and Samaria by any of the states of the world.** Jerusalem has never been the capital of any state other than the Jewish one. Palestine has never been a state after the expulsion of the Jews from it, it was only part of the various caliphates and empires that conquered this land and took it from each other. Judea is the land of the Jews; they have no other land on Earth. And **at least** this applies to those areas of **Judea and Samaria where Arabs do not live,** and which are already largely inhabited by Israelis. On what basis should these lands be considered Arab and not Jewish? There is no such reason. This is the land of the Jews, bequeathed to them by God and belonging to them legally, both as reclaimed in a just war against the aggressor, and by the Decision of the League of Nations. The Jews were already illegally deprived of 78% of the land that was intended for them according to **the decision of the Conference of the Winning Countries in San Remo in 1920**, approved by the US Congress and the League of Nations, creating an Arab state on this territory - Jordan, whose population is in the majority - those the same Arabs, "Palestinian" Arabs. In fact, they already have their own state - Jordan, and Gaza is now completely independent. They already have two independent states, why create a third? Why, in this case, the UN and the countries of the world are not fighting for the independence **of all national**

enclaves in all countries? This is considered **contrary to international norms**; such are called separatists. No one even supports the independence of Kurdistan from Turkey, Iraq, Iran and Syria, although the Kurds are a very large people, of about 40 million, who do not have their own state at all, compactly living on this land for centuries, and did not come to this land recently, like the majority Arabs to Palestine (mainly from Syria, Egypt and Lebanon). And there are 22 Arab states, with a huge territory and a huge population. To demand this only from Israel is **complete absurd** and absolutely unjust. We must not forget that the overwhelming majority of the Arabs of Palestine are newcomers, not the indigenous population, who have no right to create their own state on this primordially Jewish land and, conversely, have all the rights to return to their Arab countries, from which their fathers or grandfathers arrived (Jews from Arab countries were simply forced to leave, abandoning their property, on pain of death, they did not stand on ceremony with them). At the end of the 19th century, it was a desert, whose population was almost entirely made up of nomadic Bedouin tribes (with whom Israel still has normal relations). Only in Jerusalem, which retained a Jewish majority, and in several other small towns, did a very small number of sedentary Arabs live. Here is what Mark Twain, who was traveling in Palestine at that time, wrote: "There is not a solitary village throughout its whole extent – not for 30 miles in either direction. There are two or three small clusters of Bedouin tents, but not a single permanent habitation. One may ride 10 miles, hereabouts, and not see 10 human beings. Desolate deserts, gloomy barren mountains." When Jews came to Palestine and transformed it, made it attractive to life, created jobs, hundreds of thousands of Arabs from Arab countries poured into it. Now they are laying claim to all this land. In Israel, there are constant armed attacks and explosions, the victims of which are innocent children, old people, women, everything. A large-scale terror is being carried out against the civilian population in the hope of causing a mass exodus of Jews

103

from Israel. **The decision of the League of Nations of July 24, 1922 is currently the only document of the highest international organization that has legal force on the question of which lands should belong to the Jewish state**. The adjoining Anglo-American Declaration of 1925 is approved as **US law**. Those. The United States is the guarantor of the implementation of this decision of the League of Nations. Accordingly, **all Jewish settlements on this land are absolutely legal**. Unfortunately, Israel's right to security is incompatible with the existence of an independent Arab Palestinian state in the place where the Arab Palestinian Authority is now located. Therefore, it is necessary to expose the lie that a "peaceful settlement" will lead to peace and improve Arab attitudes towards Western countries. On the contrary, the confrontation will only escalate since it will give the Arabs much greater opportunities in the fight against Israel. Israel, as an unsinkable aircraft carrier and the only true ally in the Middle East, is needed by the West, especially America. Unlike other US allies, Israel does not require sending the military, and it spends financial assistance on the purchase of American equipment and technology, which is beneficial to the American side. Raised in the Arabs of Judea and Samaria (transmitted, thanks to monstrously false propaganda, and part of the Israeli Arabs), hatred of Jews knows no boundaries, it starts from the very young, childhood years (thanks to programs for children like "Kill a Jew") and it is monstrous. If this is not Nazism, then what is Nazism. As a result, should one of the Jews accidentally get into an Arab village or city of the Palestinian Authority, the brutal crowd of Arabs kills and lynches them (him, her) in the most terrible, most brutal way. Every time, terrible terrorist acts are carried out - attacks by Arabs, mainly from the Palestinian Authority, whole families are slaughtered, they do not spare either the elderly or young children. And recently, a wave of pogroms perpetrated by Israeli Arabs in cities with a mixed population swept across Israel. Very often terrorist attacks are organized by the authorities of the autonomy, although the latter are constantly trying to create the appearance that they are allegedly against it and even allegedly trying to prevent them, while at the same time financing terrorists imprisoned for their crimes and their families and inciting hatred. Their goal is to force the Jews to leave Israel, to destroy Israel. They do not need any state of their own, this is a lie. They want an Arab state **instead** of a Jewish state. No other solution will suit them. Moreover, in this case, they would have ceased to be constantly fed free of charge and they would have had to establish life in the territories under their control, and they know that it is practically impossible without such help and even with it - their "state" is not viable. Otherwise, such an Arab state would have existed for a long time, since 1948. And later, Arafat refused, despite the extreme, very dangerous, criminal, in my opinion, absolutely unacceptable for Israel concessions on the part of Ehud Barak. And even if, purely hypothetically, someday the Arabs of Palestine, brought up from an early age in the belief that this is their land, agree to some kind of "peace," and Israel will give them part of their land for this, it must be understood that all the same it will not lead to peace, because they see any agreements with the "infidels" only as another step towards the complete destruction of Israel. To prevent this, it is necessary to **introduce into Israeli legislation a law on the inadmissibility of the creation of an independent Arab state in any part of Judea and Samaria. And about the inadmissibility of transferring the Golan Heights to Syria**, conquered during the war against a state that committed unprovoked aggression against Israel, without which the north of Israel is almost impossible to defend. By the way, the Palestine Liberation Organization, which now exercises power in the Palestinian Authority, was created back in 1964, i.e., before the 1967 war, when there were no Jews or Israeli troops in Judea and Samaria (and in Gaza too). **What lands were they going to liberate then?** As for the religious side of the issue, **clear instructions from God about the will of this land to the Jews are contained not only in the Bible, but**

also in the Koran, although they try to hide it. **We need to make sure that all Muslims know about this.**

About the formula "two states for two peoples" imposed by the whole world on Israel, which is considered the only possible solution that should appear because of negotiations between Israel and the Palestinian Authority: If we assume that one state - Jewish - already exists, then the second state will be Arab. If we are divided along ethnic lines, which seems to be meant, then all the Israeli Arabs, of whom about two million, should be sent to the Arab state that is being created, and the Jewish settlers, about half a million, to Israel. And if divided based on the creation of states in which one of the nations (Jewish or Arab) predominates, but it is possible for a minority belonging to another of these nations to live, then the Arab inhabitants of Israel will remain in it, and the Jewish settlers - in the future Arab state. But the Arab leaders of the PA initially argue that Israel will stay with its Arabs, and the Jews of Judea and Samaria should be resettled to Israel, providing a "Judenfrei" for the future Arab state. This supposedly goes without saying, it is not negotiable. And everyone agrees with this formula? Does everyone think it's fair? Either the world has gone mad, or the anti-Semitism and selfishness of its leaders have completely clouded their minds. And this is not to mention the fact that the Arabs refuse to recognize the Jewish character of the State of Israel even in such a clearly unfair case. So, what kind of negotiations between Israel and the PA can we talk about? What should they discuss? talk about? What should they discuss? Something that can only lead to obvious, undisguised injustice towards Jews? What for? And even if there is at least one of the leaders of the civilized world who clearly says that when he speaks of "two states for two peoples," he means such injustice, it is not for nothing that they all avoid details. It is time for the leaders of Israel to stop repeating this nonsense. John Bolton: "The only logic underlying the state's demands for the Palestinian Arabs is the political imperative of Israel's adversaries, thus seeking to weaken and encircle the Jewish state, minimizing its potential to create secure borders." As Martin Sherman writes, "the attempt to put into practice the doctrine of two states has failed in the past, is impossible at the present time, and in the future carries with it outright threats and is simply extremely dangerous. The death threats inherent in the 'two states' paradigm have now become so obvious that it has become far from easy to pass calls for statehood to Palestinian Arabs as genuine concern for the welfare of the Jewish state. Therefore, it's time to send this hypocritical narrative to the dustbin of history."

So, what is Israel really supposed to do in this situation? After all, there is a fierce political and propaganda offensive by the leadership of the Palestinian Authority to denigrate and de-legitimize Israel and create an independent Arab Palestinian state in all disputed territories of Judea and Samaria as another step towards its elimination. This is their main line: Create a state and then eliminate Israel. **No further digression! Israel needs to pursue a policy of active settlement of Judea and Samaria in zone C, those lands where there are no Arabs.** The number of Jews in this zone should be such that there could not even be an assumption that they could be resettled back. But this is hardly possible without the extension of Israel's sovereignty to those lands that, undoubtedly, 100%, should belong to it, i.e., on the part of zone C, in which there are no Arabs, but there are Jewish cities and settlements, and in which Israel already exercises political and military power, so in principle this will not change anything. First, this concerns areas located near the longest border with Jordan and of strategic importance. Only the extension of Israel's sovereignty to the indicated parts of zone C can instill confidence in those who would like to settle there, and in the Jewish settlers living there, that they will not one day be expelled from these lands drenched in their blood and sweat, as happened with the

Jewish settlers in the Gaza Strip. It would also prevent the possible **loss of these lands** because of illegal, contradictory actions of the Palestinian Arabs. At the very least, the Palestinian Arabs should not be allowed to create an independent state. If Israel allows the Palestinian Arabs to create an independent state (apart from the de facto independent Gaza), there will be no Israel. And it is also impossible to allow the Arabs of Gaza to constantly shell their territory. After all, each state has the right to defend itself and, moreover, not to allow steps that would inevitably lead to its death. Any condemnation of Israel for such actions shows only the anti-Semitism of those who express such condemnation. Hatred and actions against the people of God, the people of Abraham, Moses, Jesus, will sooner or later be punished. So as Iran's leadership, which constantly threatens to "wipe Israel off the world's map", and those who support it.

By the way, here are some interesting facts about how the unreasonable element reacts to what is happening in the human world. Data from articles by Victoria Vekselman and Khaim Sokolin. At the 1982 Madrid Conference, President Bush Sr. imposed on Israel the "Territories for Peace" formula. The next day, the "storm of the century" erupted over the Atlantic and waves 15 meters high washed away the president's house in Maine. On June 8, 2001, President Bush Jr.'s envoy, Tenet, brought the so-called "road map" to Israel. On the same day, Tropical Storm "Allison" hit the president's home state of Texas, raged for 5 days, and ended when Tenet left Israel. The damage amounted to $ 7 billion. In May 1967, in the days when the leadership of the USSR persuaded Egypt and Syria, armed by them, to attack Israel to wipe it off the face of the Earth, as their leaders openly declared, the largest catastrophe broke out on the territory of Russia, the consequences of which have not yet been eliminated. Lake Karachay, the largest open-air storage of radioactive waste, suddenly became shallow because of an unprecedented drought, and in early June, just in the days of the Six Day War, equally unexpected and unprecedented squall winds lifted bottom sediments into the air and carried them across a vast territory with a population in tens (and maybe hundreds, there is no exact data) of thousands of people. Scientists call Lake Karachay "Ten Chernobyls." The radiation level in the lake is 100 times higher than that of Chernobyl. In the 17th century, Khmelnitsky's Cossacks killed a huge number of Jews. They especially committed atrocities in one village, in which all Jews, including women and children, were herded into the synagogue, and burned alive. Approximately 350 years later, it was at this place that the fourth block of the Chernobyl nuclear power plant, built on it, exploded. And Stalin's death just on the eve of the prepared deportation of Jews to Siberia and the Arctic, which would inevitably end with the death of the majority of the people, a new Holocaust?

There are many similar facts, only the brightest are given here. Is this all coincidence?

LIFE AFTER DEATH

There are several compelling facts that can be considered evidence of the existence of the soul and life after death. But there is no hard scientific evidence yet. However, there are several attempts to explain these facts precisely as evidence of the existence of life after death on the part of scientists, from a scientific point of view. But all these are only hypotheses, perhaps correct, or perhaps not. They do not provide rigorous proofs of the existence of the soul. So, this question is still open and is a matter of faith.

Consider these facts. The first group of them is associated with **the memories of those who have been in a state of clinical death**, when the heart is no longer beating, but the brain has not yet died. Many of them saw themselves from the outside, heard the conversations of doctors and medical staff when they tried to bring them back to life, saw their actions, felt very light, flying under the ceiling, some even seemed to move through the walls into neighboring rooms and saw them. Then they were flying down some long corridor towards the distant light. Some saw a bright light at the end of the flight and met their relatives and acquaintances who had died earlier. Others immediately went on a journey along the "corridor," bypassing the stage of monitoring their body and medical staff. These memories are the foundation of theories about the presence of people's souls "in heaven," as a rule, in God's kingdom, and that spiritualistic contacts are possible with them.

Another group of facts is associated **with people's memories of what they could not see and know in any way**. This mostly happens under hypnosis. But in children it happens even without hypnosis. For example, a resident of Australia, under hypnosis, saw and described some room where something important was lying, unfortunately, I now no longer remember what. He indicated the exact location in one of the cities of England. And this thing was found - because of excavations in this place. She was in a layer that is 500 years old. That is, a person saw what happened 500 years ago and, in a country, far from his place of residence, in the country in which his ancestors were supposed to live. And there are many such cases. How to explain them? They are the basis for the theory of the transmigration of souls, that after death the soul of a person moves into the body of another, newly born person. As a rule, not immediately after death, but after some time, sometimes very long. It is not known where the soul is located between the periods of being in the human body, there may be different assumptions. In particular, many believe that souls are "in heaven."

Another explanation for the facts of such memories is given by Buddhism (its main directions), which recognizes the chain of reincarnations, but rejects the presence of a soul. For more details see below, in the chapter "Table of existing and potential religions." I will only say that it is not entirely clear and does not inspire confidence in me personally.

There is also a theory about the afterlife, which has purely religious grounds, without confirmation by real facts.

In my opinion, the only real hope for life after death is given only by the **existence of the soul**. This is a criterion in the selection of those ideas about the afterlife that can correspond to reality. Everything else is absolutely untrustworthy and has absolutely no evidence.

By the way, many experiments were carried out to establish the presence of a soul by the weight lost by a person at the time of death. The bed with the dying man was weighed on an ultra-precise balance. The results varied greatly, from 2 to 25 grams, most often from 5 to 23, but the difference was always, and usually came abruptly, at the very moment of death.

My task is similar to the previous one, when existing and potentially possible religions were analyzed from the point of view of available data and common sense. Now you and I must analyze on the same grounds (available data and common sense) **the existing and potentially possible concepts of life after death** and determine which of them, in principle, can correspond to the truth and which cannot.

So, let's consider the existing and potentially possible concepts of life after death.

The first and main group of concepts of life after death are those that are associated with religions based on **faith in God**. And in principle also those who believe in the existence of many gods. There are an overwhelming majority of such religions. That's why I called this group the main one.

1. Let's start with a purely religious concept. This is the version that people die, there is no soul, but after a certain time, they will supposedly be "awakened" by God - those who deserve it for the subsequent eternal life in paradise - in heaven, in God's kingdom, or on Earth, and the rest - for a short time, with their subsequent killing, so that they regretted that they sinned. Moreover, this is not confirmed by any facts. It is difficult and even impossible to imagine that billions of people from the depths of millennia will be recreated from nothing, from some long-term decayed bones or the ashes of burnt bodies, sometimes scattered in the wind, or simply from ideas about these people, about each of these billions preserved in memory of God. In my opinion, **this is pure fantasy, which has no chance of being true**. Especially striking is the belief in recreating a huge number of people for a short moment, only so that they regret their bad behavior, followed by their mass murder. As if for God to recreate billions of people is a trifle, worthless. I think even for God, no matter what supernatural abilities He may have, recreating billions of people from practically nothing cannot be so easy as to do it for a moment. Absurd!

2. The most common of the existing is the concept of Jesus Christ about heaven and hell. As I have already said, there can be no **eternal** punishment with our such short earthly life. It is impossible to imagine eternal punishment, eternal torment. Moreover, given by our heavenly Father, God. Common sense revolts against this. This concept is impossible not to **reject**. Although almost all types of Christianity are committed to it.

3. The third concept is **about heaven**, "God's kingdom," but **combined** not with eternal hell, but **with a temporary punishment in "purgatory" for those who deserve it**. Most go straight to heaven. The severity and duration of punishment depends on the severity of a person's sins in earthly life. Such a theory may indeed be true. If you believe in God, then there is no reason not to believe in a just temporary punishment for sins. In this case, in the afterlife. On the other hand, the soul is an extremely rarefied structure; it is unlikely that it can experience pain. Therefore, I do not reject this concept completely, 100%, but I consider the likelihood of compliance with its truth extremely **unlikely**.

4. The fourth concept is belief **in both God and the chain of reincarnations**, i.e., a series of transmigration of the **soul** into the bodies of newly born babies. In my opinion, **such a possibility cannot be ruled out**, it is confirmed by people's memories of what they could not see and know in any way. In religions based on faith in God, for example, in one of the directions of Judaism, the fate of the soul is decided by God. Paradise at the end of the path is not excluded - after many reincarnations, as a result of improving her "quality," her ascent to perfection.

5. I would like to propose a **new** concept related to God. This is a belief **both in God and in the fact that the soul exists, most likely, in**

paradise, but not infinitely. The soul is not immortal. The length of its life depends on how much it is burdened with grave sins, i.e., how pure and good it is or how sinful and bad it is. All this is determined by God.

6. And one more new concept is the belief **in God and in the fact that the punishment of a person for sins is carried out by God during this life on Earth, i.e., everyone who sins seriously** pays for it sooner or later with his health - diseases, sometimes premature death (premature for him, regardless of the general indicators). However, it is usually very diffi- cult to trace such a connection. You can call such a belief **Sadducism**. This includes the version that our souls after the death of the body live for **a very short time** and die within about forty days.

Now about those concepts of life after death that are not related to God, but, nevertheless, are related to the punishment for sins. These beliefs exist in religions that deny or question the existence of God.

7. Buddhism is a belief in **a chain of reincarnations**, by which in this case we mean a series of rebirths (transformations) of a person into newly born babies, which is confirmed by people's memories of what they could not see and know in any way. In this case, the existence of the soul is rejected. Paradise at the end of the path is not excluded - after many rein- carnations, as a result of human improvement. In Buddhism, into whom a person will be reborn depends on how a person lived his earthly life, how sinful he was, but at the expense of what forces, in the absence of God, and how, in the absence of a soul, it is not entirely clear. This is supposedly the law of nature. I think this belief is too fantastic, unsupported by anything and should be **rejected**.

8. This is actually an existing belief, let's call it **Soul Buddhism**, in the chain of reincarnations (samsara), but in this case it is a series of trans- migration of the **soul** into the bodies of newly born babies, confirmed by people's memories of what they could not see and know in any way, and then that the more sinful you are, the "blacker" your soul, the worse initial conditions you will find yourself in (born into a poor, dysfunctional family). At the end of the path, after gradual correction and "ascent" of the soul, paradise is possible. The periods of being in the bodies of people alternate with the periods between the invasions of earthly bodies. This includes some of the directions of Buddhism, Judaism, and the main directions of Hinduism.

9. I would like to propose **a new concept based on the idea of reincarnation** and, accordingly, a new potentially possible religion, **New Buddhism**, according to which this is really a law of nature, which consists in the fact that there is a huge **competition** between souls for the opportunity to inhabit the human body. The human soul does not contain much of what has a body that is perfectly adapted for life, and therefore, I think, it drags out a miserable existence. The law of nature is that it is much more difficult for "black" souls, weighed down by grave sins, to penetrate the bodies of newborn babies than for "light" souls, and they stay in such an unenviable state for a long time, and some, perhaps, fail at all and they die. In other words, the life of the soul is limited, and it can perish if it does not have time to settle in the human body within a certain time. At the end of the path, because of the progress of the soul, an almost endless paradise is possible.

10. It is clear that people really want to hope for a better future, for immortality and a permanent life in pleasure. But we cannot deny other options, which are not so rosy. I would also like to propose a very real **new** concept, I called it **Langs**, according to which the soul exists, and, possibly, in paradise, "in heaven," but **not infinitely. The soul is not immortal**. The length of its life depends **on how much she is weighed down by grave sins** and how pure and good it is. This is the law of nature. Perhaps we are talking about very significant periods, about thousands of years. But

it is possible that they are much shorter or longer. I would be glad if this period was thousands of years. But if the duration of its life depends on how much energy the body managed to accumulate during its life, which is most likely, then we are talking about terms of one hundred to two hundred years, hardly more.

11. Scientology puts forward a version that the soul, after the death of the body, flies to another planet and is not only immortal, but also acquires a permanent new body there. It is highly doubtful. **I reject it.**

And the last group of concepts. **Three** are also **new**, proposed concepts based on the religion of **Karmaism**. Those options in which punishments for sins (and, possibly, rewards for good deeds) in the absence of God are carried out already during this life, according to this religion, at the expense of some other forces, most likely from our subconscious mind. In this case, no punishment occurs in the afterlife.

12. Karmaism - Langs. The concept that souls are not immortal live, perhaps, **in paradise, and for a very long, but limited time, approximately the same for all people.**

13. Karmaism - Samsara. The concept of a **chain of reincarnations** is not according to the "quality"" of the soul, but due to random circumstances, most likely, with the closest baby being born. Perhaps with paradise at the end of the road, after a certain number of reincarnations.

14. Karmaism - Paradise. The belief that souls are immortal, and since the punishment has already been, in the future, the souls of all people go to **heaven**, for an almost infinite time, and there is no purgatory (and, moreover, hell).

As you can see, there are **9** quite realistic options: 3 for those who believe in God, 3 for those who believe in life after death even in the absence of God, and 3 for those who, in the absence of God, believe in punishment even with this life (Karmaism). At the same time, the existence of the soul **does not yet prove that it is eternal** and after the death of the body it is in sufficiently comfortable conditions. Moreover, its very existence can only be spoken of with one or another, possibly high, degree of probability. I do not exclude the existence of a soul, and I even think that there are very high chances for this. But excessive optimism is hardly justified. Therefore, the concept of **Karma - Langs 12** is closest to me and seems most likely, second, **Karmaism - Samsara 13**, **New Buddhism 9, and Soul - Buddhism 8**, and for those who believe in God, a new concept **5** (the life span of the soul - by the will of God) and the existing concept **4** (reincarnation by the will of God). It is very naive to expect a very good, ideal future in paradise. The only thing we can count on, in which we can be certain to a certain extent, is that the **soul exists**. All other options have not yet been confirmed and should be discarded. So, you can't be overly optimistic. Excessive optimism leads to such ugly phenomena as suicides, who believe that they will go to heaven so soon, and as suicide bombers who kill innocent people, believing that they will receive a special reward in heaven for this. But such hopes are absolutely groundless. I want to say to such people: Be grateful and happy if the soul really exists and at least some kind of continuation awaits us. However, **it may be very long and not devoid of pleasantness**. And this is very inspiring. But everything else is unwarranted fantasies. As in the case of religions, it is the most fantastic and unlikely options that have the largest number of supporters. Too many people want to hear only what is associated with science fiction, with miracles; and the more and more amazing the miracles, the stronger their faith. First of all, I try to follow common sense.

When I talk about the immortality of the soul, I mean that it will live for an extremely long time, millions and even, perhaps, hundreds of millions of years. It is hardly possible to talk about complete immortality, endless existence. Humanity in general is threatened with death in about 500 million to a billion years, when the Sun increases its luminosity to such an extent that life on Earth due to extremely high temperatures will become impossible, and the oceans will evaporate. And if humanity cannot move to a more distant planet, it will perish. At the very least, reincarnation will become impossible. And then the Sun will increase so much that it will most likely engulf the Earth's orbit, and it will disappear. But 500 million years is such a huge time that we shouldn't be discouraged.

If we consider the matter on a large scale, no matter what forces life after death depends on, you get the following options:

1. Life in paradise has a very significant, but limited time depending on the severity of sins, or almost endless, but after punishment on Earth.

2. The chain of reincarnations - after the punishment carried out on Earth, either in a good or bad version of reincarnation, depending on the severity of sins, or the same by the will of God, with a possible paradise at the end.

I would very much like the first option to be true, when the personality is not lost, especially in the option when the punishment is carried out on Earth, and then a very long, possibly almost infinite life in "paradise" awaits us (at least in a state where no one can hurt us), but I must admit that both options have about the same chance of being true.

In both cases, we can only guess about the duration of life in paradise or the chain of reincarnations. There are three options here.

The first one is pessimistic: the Soul outside the body does not have the ability to absorb energy, therefore, the duration of its existence depends entirely on the amount of energy that it received from the body, and is very small, most likely up to forty days.

The second, and most likely, I think. The soul outside the body has the ability to absorb energy, but to a much lesser extent than in the human body (in relation to the amount that it needs to exist). Therefore, the duration of its life depends both on the amount of energy it constantly absorbs, and on the energy that it acquired during its life in the human body. In this variant, I think after the death of the body, the soul lives for another 100 years on average, as long as it has enough of the accumulated energy reserve for a person's life. And if there is a possibility of reincarnation, then this is only one reincarnation, and even then, if you are lucky. I am such a pessimist. But on the other hand, I consider such options quite realistic and reasonable. They are based on facts about the existence of the soul. In my opinion, these facts are connected not simply with some phenomena in the human brain during the period of dying, but are a reflection of reality, i.e., the fact that the soul at such moments is separated from the body. Another thing is how long a soul can exist without a body. Here, in principle, various options are possible, from a few days to almost immortality. I think the latter is hardly realistic, and just a few days is also unlikely, as that is too pessimistic. Most likely, in the process of living in the body, the soul acquires a certain level of energy, sufficient for its rather long subsequent existence. And the lifetime of about 100 - 150 years is closest to reality. This is if the punishment for sins comes during life, as the new religion of Karmaism says. If it is carried out after the death of a person, then, accordingly, this period can vary widely, perhaps from 50 to 250 years. Serious sins of a person affect the state of the soul and reduce its ability to survive, while good deeds, on the contrary, increase this ability. This is what the new religion of Langs is talking about, a variant of it that I have called Real Langs.

The third option, the life of the soul for millions of years, or even immortality (in which I do not believe), can only be associated with the ability of the soul to acquire enough energy for life throughout its life. As for the variant of the chain of reincarnations, which is possible only if the second or third variants are true, it can be quite long, but, as I already wrote, it is hardly more than 500 million years because this is most likely the maximum life span of humanity. There will be no people - there will be no one to inhabit. And in our time, about 8 billion people live on Earth, and in total during the existence of mankind there were about 80 billion of them. This confirms my idea that there are always more souls than people, and there is fierce competition between them for places in human bodies.

TABLE OF EXISTING AND POTENTIALLY POSSIBLE RELIGIONS

As I already mentioned, when you get acquainted with existing religions and philosophies, it is surprising that there is only one "unifying" religion (Baha'ism), while such a unifying religion should be generated by each of the "basic" religions, starting with the second. This prompted me to try to create a generalized, generalized picture of existing and potential religions. There is no complete knowledge yet. This shows the necessity of the existence of unifying religions, each of which "contains" a number of similar views and is placed in the bottom line of the table. The religions listed below can be called **combined** or conditional. They are not divided depending on how the afterlife is represented by a particular religion (since sometimes there are different ideas about this within one religion). The division goes only depending on **the ideas about God** (or, for some religions, about the gods, or about other Higher Powers) and His (their) existence, **from the relationship to Jesus Christ** (from the first to the 15th) and **from the source** (general for all 200 commandments of the Torah, 225 commandments that are the minimum for Jews, 613 commandments of the Torah from the list of Maimonides or all commandments of the Torah, books of Judaism, Buddhism, Hinduism, Koran, etc.).

After each of the above 25 religions (or rather, in most cases, groups of close religions) and 4 philosophies (depending on their attitude to religion and humanism - the fulfillment of the laws of morality), its number is given in the general table. New religions and philosophies are emphasized. Note: Those religions that are misanthropic and use violent methods, terror, or set themselves the task of conquering by any means, including violent methods, world domination, in particular, Radical Islam, Satanists, etc., **in this table are not included and are not considered here**. This includes only humanistic religions that correspond to high moral principles and educate their parishioners on them. This table is:

J	Pr	Env	MC	EC	C	NBM	PM	Hin	P	Pl	F	K	Ag	At
1	2	4	6	8	10	12	14	16	18	20	22	24	25	27
	3	5	7	9	11	13	15	17	19	21	23	25	27	29
	NJ	N	B	Bt	Bc	Ba	Un	Uv	T	Inf	Pro	Ua	Uph	AH

1. Existing "Basic" Religion (EBR) **Judaism (1). Belief in the One and Indivisible God. Jesus' relationship with God is rejected**. For a more detailed description of it, see above, in the chapter "Judaism, Prophetism, Invoism, Messianic Christianity," part "Judaism." In the same column, the religions are **Injudaism** and **Light-Injudaism** (see above, in the same chapter in the part "Judaism" and in the chapter "Injudaism"). 2. The existing "basic" religion (EBR) **Prophetism (2)** (Prophet-Injudaism or In-Prophetism). **The same, but Jesus is recognized as a prophet of God**. For a more detailed description of it, see above, in the chapter "Judaism, Prophetism, Envoism, Messianic Christianity," the part "Prophetism," and in the chapter "Injudaism." Another version of it - the religion of **Prophet-Judaism** (Judaism-Prophetism) - for those who consider it necessary to

fulfill all the commandments of the Torah or the minimum required 225. For a more detailed description of it, see above, in the same chapter "Judaism, Prophetism, Invoism, Messianic Christianity," part "Prophetism." 3. New "Unifying" Religion (NUR) **New Judaism (3)** (New Injudaism, General Injudaism, Nujudaism, Mosheism, Moseism, Bivarism, Bivariate Religion). It unites Judaism - Injudaism and Prophetism. Recognizes **both the described options of the relationship to Jesus Christ as possible**. For a more detailed description of it, see above, in the chapter "New Judaism" and in the chapter "Injudaism." In the same column, the religion is **General Judaism** (United Judaism, Ujuism, Broad-Judaism, United Judaism, Common Judaism). For a description of it, see above, in the same chapter "Judaism, Prophetism, Envoism, **Messianic Christianity,**" part of "Judaism." 4. The existing "basic" religion (EBR) Messianic Christianity (6) (Messianism, Judeo-Christianity). **Recognizes Jesus as the Envoy of God and the future Messiah**. For a more detailed description of it, see above, in the chapter "Judaism, Prophetism, Envoism, Messianic Christianity," the part "Messianic Christianity," and in the chapter "Injudaism." In the same column, the religion is **Messianic Judaism** (Judeo-Christianity). For a more detailed description of it, see above, in the same chapter "Judaism, Prophetism, Envoism, Messianic Christianity," part "Messianic Christianity." 5. New "basic" religion **Envoism (4)** - filling the "blank spot" in the basic religions between Prophetism and Messianic Christianity. **Recognizes Jesus as the Envoy of God**. For a more detailed description of it, see above, in the chapter "Judaism, Prophetism, Envoism, Messianic Christianity," the part "Envoism," and in the chapter "Injudaism." Its other version is **Envoy-Judaism** (Judaism-Envoism) - for those who consider it necessary to fulfill all the commandments of the Torah or the minimum required 225. For a more detailed description of it, see above, in the same chapter "Judaism, Prophetism, Envoism, Messianic Christianity," part "Envoism." 6. New "uniting" religion (NUR) **Newarism (5)** (Truarism,

New Religion, Newism, Nurism, Trivarism, Three-Variant Religion). **Recognizes the possibility of three options: Jesus Christ is not connected with God, he is a prophet of God, he is an Envoy of God**. Combines all religions from (1) to (4). For a more detailed description of it, see above, in the chapter "Newarism" and in the chapter "Injudaism." Another version of it - **Judaism-Newarism** (Newarism - Judaism) - for those who consider it necessary to fulfill all the commandments of the Torah or the minimum required 225. For a more detailed description of it, see above, in the chapter "Newarism." In the same column, the religion is **Prophet-Newarism**, which unites Newarism with Prophetism, cutting off traditional Judaism. 7. New unifying religion **Bibleism (7)** (Biblism, Biblicalism, General Unitarism, Religion of the Indivisible God, RIG). Combines all religions from (1) to (6). **It recognizes the possibility of four options: Jesus Christ is not connected with God, he is a prophet of God, he is an Envoy of God, he will come as the Messiah**. For a more detailed description of it, see above, in the chapter "Bibleism" and in the chapter "Injudaism." Another option is **Judaism - Bibleism** (Bibleism - Judaism) - for those who consider it necessary to fulfill all the commandments of the Torah or the minimum required 225. The option connecting Bibleism with Prophetism, that is, cutting off Judaism and Injudaism - **Prophet-Bibleism** (Prophet-Biblism). The variant of **Envoy - Bibleism** is not excluded, which cuts off both Judaism and Prophetism. 8. EBR **Evangelical Christianity (8)**. Includes most areas of **Protestantism**. Considers Jesus Christ not only the Messiah, but also God Himself, or rather, God the Son, - simultaneously a separate person and a part of God, i.e., part of the Trinity, which includes God the Father, God the Son and God the Spirit. (i.e., God did not create Jesus). Considers the New Testament as a continuation of the Old Testament, and the re-creation of Israel as a sign of the imminent arrival of the Messiah. Supports Israel and considers it necessary to build the Third Temple to ensure the coming of the Messiah. In principle, Pentecostals, the

124

Oneness who do not believe in the Trinity, but consider Jesus to be God Himself, who descended to Earth, can also be attributed to this group. 9. NUR Bibliotheism **(9).** It unites, at least, Judaism, New Judaism, Newarism and Bibleism, and in fact (as possible options) all religions based on the Bible from Judaism (Injudaism) to Evangelical Christianity, i.e., all religions from (1) to (8). Emphasizes faith in God, and in relation to Jesus Christ considers any of the above options possible, including Jesus - God as part of the Trinity. Also considers the New Testament a continuation of the Old Testament, and the re-creation of Israel and the future construction of the Temple as signs of the imminent arrival of the Messiah. 10. EBR Christianity **(10).** Includes **Catholicism** and **Orthodoxy**, possibly some areas of **Protestantism**. Like Gospel Christianity, it considers Jesus Christ not only the Messiah, but also God - the Son, part of the Trinity. The belief, however, is that the New Testament replaced the invalid Old Testament, leaving only the Ten Commandments, and even then, without keeping the Sabbath. Christianity and Evangelical Christianity is monotheism, but, unlike all previous religions, it is not strict monotheism, but **only a kind of** monotheism - it is based on the Trinity invented by people, which is not in the Bible, on the statement about the possibility of God to have several "persons." 11. NUR **Bibliocentrism (11).** It unites, as possible options, all Bible-based religions from Judaism (Injudaism) to Christianity, i.e., all religions from (1) to (10). Emphasizes faith in God, and in relation to Jesus Christ considers any of the above options possible, including Jesus - God as part of the Trinity. 12. EBR **Non-Biblical Monotheism (12).** Common name for non-biblical monotheistic religions. This includes **Moderate Islam** (New Islam), which actually exists in the minds of many Muslims, which includes peaceful Muslims, for example, the majority of residents of Muslim countries formed from the republics of the former USSR, many of those who profess Sufi and secular Islam, declaring Muhammad (Mohammed) the main and last prophet of the One God, but rejecting aggressiveness and the doctrine of jihad against all "infidels." These are those who honor the commandment "do not kill" existing in the Koran, and not only in relation to Muslims. This also includes the existing religions **Sikkhism**, - the doctrine of the One God, present everywhere (dissolved in space), combined with faith in reincarnation, and **Yezidism (Yazidism)**, which presupposes the presence of several (seven) angels created by God as their helpers. **13.** The existing "unifying" religion of **Baha'ism** (13) unites in fact Non-Biblical Monotheism and Prophetism. He considers Jesus a prophet among other prophets, including Krishna, Abraham, Moses, Zoroaster, Buddha, Mohammed, Baba and Baha'u'llah. Variations of Baha'ism are also possible: **General Baha'ism** (United Baha'ism), combining Non-Biblical Monotheism and Prophetic Biblicalism (combining Biblical and Prophetic), New Baha'ism, combining Non-Biblical Monotheism and New Judaism, **Strict Baha'ism**, excluding Buddha, Krishna and Zoroaster from the number of prophets contradicting monotheism, and **General Monotheism**, uniting all who believe in One God (all religions from (1) to (12). 14. EBR **Poly-Monotheism (14)** (Dualism), including **Zoroastrianism**, which speaks of the existence of God-created (the Main Creator God), who has the opportunity to manifest in this world, as his assistants several (six) other gods, almost as powerful, and **Mormonism**, which considers Jesus Christ to be such a helper god. Here (to Zoroastrianism and Mormonism) I propose to attach a new religion, which I called **Numberism**, which believes that God carries out judgment on people with numerous assistants, whom He created and many of whom surpass people in their abilities and from this point of view are also gods (only you don't need to idolize them and pray to them), and God Himself organizes and controls this process, connecting Directly in special cases. 15. NUR **Unitism (15)** unites all religions from (1) to (14), i.e., all types of monotheism and Poly-Monotheism. Honors the same prophets as Baha'i (see above). 16. EBR **Hinduism (16).** An extreme version of loose monotheism, in fact a mixture of monotheism and polytheism. Assumes the presence of many (approximately two thousand) gods. The main gods are, depending on the direction (there are several of them), mainly Vishnu, Shiva, Krishna and Shakti. All gods are manifestations of the One God - the Creator, who Himself does not have the ability to manifest in this world as such, but only through other gods or through people, but not as the Main God. Therefore, many consider Hinduism to be a monotheistic religion. But, according to many other religious scholars, Hinduism is actually a belief in many gods, polytheism, in fact, contrary to monotheistic religions. And the fate of people is not necessarily decided by the gods, it is only known that they depend on the "Karma" of a person - the sum of his merits and sins. Conventionally, in order not to lengthen the table of religions, this group can also include the almost disappeared predecessor of Hinduism, **Brahmanism**, from the left, which spoke absolutely clearly about the invisible Main God - the Creator and denies the possibility of another "main" god, which can really be considered an extreme type of monotheism. In any case, it includes belief in the chain of reincarnations, **samsara**, i.e., in a series of rebirths of a person after death in the body of another newly born person (or, according to a number of directions, another being). 17. NUR **Universalism (17)** unites all religions from (1) to (16), i.e., all kinds of monotheism and Hinduism. 18. EBR **Polytheism (18)**, i.e., belief in many gods. There is ancient **Paganism, Shintoism, Jainism,** and **Polytheistic types of Buddhism, Hinduism and Taoism**. 19. NUR **Theism (19)** (Supremism) unites all religions from Judaism to Polytheism, based on belief in the **One God or gods** that are fundamentally different from humans or humanoid aliens (as creatures of approximately the same type as a person, even if they have reached significantly higher level of development), i.e., all monotheistic and polytheistic religions from (1) to (18). 20. Existing "basic" religion (EBR) **Planetism (20).** This is a belief in the existence of a developed **Extraterrestrial Civilization** that influences our destinies. Of the existing religions, this is **Realism** with its own specific characteristics. It does not exclude the possibility of the existence of **aliens** that are fundamentally different from humans or humanoid aliens (built on a different basis). **Mono-Planetism** is also possible, combining belief in an alien civilization with belief in God as the main of the practically immortal aliens influencing us (at least, as the main one on Earth). Those. one of the possible options is that God, who rescued the Jews from slavery and gave the Ten Commandments and the Torah, was a representative of an alien civilization. Perhaps He called himself God - the Creator to increase his influence on people, so that people fulfill His requirements, but in fact He did not create our world alone. 21. Uniting all previous religions from (1) to (20), including Planetism, the **Influism** religion **(21).** The belief that humanity is not alone, that there are powerful **intelligent forces** (One God, with or without helpers, or a group of gods, or an advanced alien civilization) that decide our destinies. Other types of Influism are possible, including only a part of the previous religions, for example, **Influism - New Judaism, Influism-Prophetism, Influism - Bibleism**, etc. any of the previous religions as possible options. 22. EBR **Futurism (22),** i.e., belief in an afterlife even in the absence of God. It includes **Buddhism** and the very specific religion of **Scientology**, which is difficult to attribute to any specific group and which seems to me unlikely, so I will not talk about it in detail. **Buddhism** is a very deep and very interesting religious and philosophical system. The main thing in the **religious part of Buddhism** that interests us in this case is the belief in rebirth after death in the body of a newly born person (reincarnation, samsara), and the chain of reincarnations may even be endless or ending in "nirvana" after many reincarnations. And this is not a movement of the soul - the presence of a soul is denied. Buddhism believes that the future of a person, in this case, in the body of another person, in the body of which newborn he will be reborn (from which parents), depends on how he lives (from his

"Karma"). Modern Buddhism denies the presence of gods and, in general, external rational influence, or at most does not outright exclude the possibility of such. Buddhism believes that the soul does not exist, and the rebirth of a person in another body occurs in a different way. They compare this process with the process of lighting one candle from another, burning, and the stream of consciousness acts as a fire. Because rebirth into another person occurs immediately after death. All this is hard to believe. I think there may be a new religion in this group, which I called **Soul Buddhism**, which speaks of a chain of transmigration of the soul, alternating with periods when the soul is not in the human body, but lives separately. I think there may be a new religion in this group, which I called **New Buddhism**, developing this trend. It assumes intense competition between the souls of the dead for the very opportunity to move into the body of a newly born baby and live a full-blooded earthly life. But the "blacker" the soul, the more difficult it is for it to carry this out, up to the complete impossibility of this. And the soul without a body, due to the almost complete lack of opportunities to absorb the energy necessary for life (the human body is an almost ideal "device" for this), drags out a miserable existence and eventually perishes. There may also exist a new religion **Langs** (Langsism), - the belief in the existence of the soul after the death of the body in paradise, but not forever, but for a limited time, depending on how grave a person's sins are in his earthly life - "black" souls live less, "light" - longer, and the difference can be very, very significant. And the version of **Real Langs** defines the approximate life span of a soul, depending on the severity of sins, more modestly - in a wide range from 10 to 250 years, explaining that the soul lives after the death of the body if it has enough of the reserve accumulated for a person's life energy. And it depends on the totality of good and bad deeds of a person. 23. A new religion uniting the previous religions, as possible variants, or part of them, the religion of **Prolongism (23).** The belief in the afterlife, no matter which version, not

129

only in Buddhism, is the main thing, and the presence of God (gods) is questionable. But it recognizes the need to pray to God. And the quality of the afterlife depends on how you have lived your earthly life, on whether you have sinned. The most serious sin is murder. 24. The new "basic" religion is **Karmaism (24).** The belief that **a person's future depends on how he lives** (on his "Karma"), and **the punishment comes during this life**, i.e., our future does not depend on external intelligent forces - this is the law of nature (however, it is possible that the mechanism of its execution is established by God (Higher powers), but without any further influence on our lives by Him (them). The punishment for sins is not obvious in this life, because it usually comes too late for us to catch a connection between them, but it is there - a person who does not observe the laws of morality sooner or later begins to get sick and dies sooner. In other words, **sins are one of the causes of diseases and deaths** - most likely, far from the only one, natural causes have not been canceled either. In this case, it is most likely incorrect to make a comparison between people, it's all very individual – often, this person could live longer or be healthier if he were better, did not violate the norms of morality. There are also certain arguments in favor of this, related to the properties of water, of which we consist of more than 70%, with its changing its structure in case of bad human behavior, i.e., most likely, the **subconscious** mind is acting here, or some other mechanisms unrelated to external intelligent forces (except, perhaps, our own souls in the afterlife, if they exist), as well as the influence (anger, envy) **of other people**. And punishment, I am sure, depends not on axioms, not on what we believe, but on how we live. The question of the afterlife is open. To see more about this religion, see above the chapter on **Karmaism**. A variant of this religion is also possible, Karma-Futurism, combining faith in punishment for sins already in this life with faith in the afterlife (already without punishment). There are different options here: **Karma - Samsara**, according to which there is a chain of soul reincarnations, but at the same time, most likely, the soul inhabits the body of just the person who is born closest in location, **Karma - Paradise**, talking about the existence of all souls in paradise indefinitely, and **Karma - Langs**, talking about the existence of all souls in paradise, but the same time for all, albeit significant, but not infinite. 25. A new religion uniting all the previous religions, as possible variants, the religion of **Uarism (25)** (**United Religion**, United Punishism). At the same time, the combination of **Uarism** with **Futurism** is **Punishism**, and if Uarism unites **parts** of these religions, it is a combination of **Punishism**. There are many possible options depending on which religions to unite (**Punishism - New Judaism, Punishism - Prophetism, Punishism - Newarism, Punishism - Bibleism, Punishism - Prolongism** etc.). The belief in punishment for sins, in the fact that a person's future, and not necessarily only in the afterlife, but perhaps already in this life, depends on how he lives. There are some forces that affect us, although we do not know their nature, whether they are intelligent (One God, with or without helpers) or not, perhaps it is our own subconscious. About this religion, see also the chapter **Uarism** above. 26. The old "basic" philosophy (OBP) of **Agnosticism (26)**. The existing philosophical trend uniting those who do not reject religions does not exclude those certain religions which may correspond to the truth, but doubts it, are not sure of the reality of their ideas, i.e., it is something between faith and unbelief. There may also be **Agnosticism - Uphism**, for those agnostics who believe that if we do not deny the possibility of punishment for sins, then we should live observing moral norms. 27. New Unifying Philosophy (NUP) **Uphism (27)** (United Philosophy, General Philosophy). It unites believers and agnostics - Uphists. For a description of it, see the chapter on Uphism. 28. OBP **Atheism (28)**, - disbelief neither in God, nor in any other Higher Powers and their influence on our life, nor in the existence of an afterlife, nor in punishment for sins. Compliance or non-compliance with moral norms depends in this case only on the moral qualities of a person. A combination of **Atheism and Active Humanism** is also possible (see below). 29. NUP **Active Humanism (29)**. This is a philosophy that unites everyone, both believers and non-believers, in the understanding that it is necessary to be guided by truly **humanistic principles**, as well as **actively resist evil**, otherwise it can defeat and turn us into slaves. As Judaism says, "Whoever is merciful to the cruel is cruel to the merciful." I will give the table again. In total, there are **25** religions in it: **13 "basic"** religions or groups of close religions - **11** "basic" **existing** religions and **2 new** religions **(4, 24)**, as well as **12 "unifying"** religions, - **1 existing (13)** "unifying" religion and **11 new** "unifying" religions. There are also **4** philosophies - **2 existing "basic"** and **2 new** "unifying." Here is a complete view of the table:

J	Pr	Env	MC	EC	C	NBM	PM	Hin	P	Pl	F	K	Ag	At
1	2	4	6	8	10	12	14	16	18	20	22	24	25	27
	3	5	7	9	11	13	15	17	19	21	23	25	27	29
	NJ	N	B	Bt	Bc	Ba	Un	Uv	T	Inf	Pro	Ua	Uph	AH

The embracing religions (5) to (23) do not have to include absolutely all of the previous ones, exceptions are possible. For example, **Influism (21)** may not include **Hinduism (16), Non-Biblical Monotheism (12)**, or **Christianity (10)** as possible options, and **Uarism (Punishism) (25)**, in addition to those listed, may not also include **Polytheism (18) and Planetism (20)**. Religions are possible that combine any of the monotheistic religions from (1) to (13) with **Planetism (20)**, when aliens are considered as one of the tools of God (possibly, along with angels, or with people selected for this after their earthly death, turned into angels - but this is most likely a fantasy), and with **Karmaism (24)** (also as an instrument of God). According to the degree of conviction and involvement in religion, any of the religions can be combined with **Uphism (27)** or with **Agnosticism (26)**. Each of the religions from **Judaism (1)** to **Baha'ism (13)** is connected - or not connected - with **Numberism**, - according to how God exercises judgment on people (Himself, or with numerous helpers, or by introducing into nature a mechanism for automatically determining the fate of a person during his life on Earth - beforehand, before the final judgment, or without it). Connections of religions are also possible, "cutting off" those that are located at the beginning of the table, for example, the connection **of Newarism (5), Bibleism (7),** or **Bibliocentrism (11)** with **Prophetism (2)** (cutting off Judaism with Injudaism), etc. It is also possible to unite the proposed unifying religions - **New Judaism** with **Newarism**, emphasizing the priority of **New Judaism** over **Newarism**, but not a complete rejection of the latter as a possible option in principle, similarly - for the unions **Judaism - General Judaism, New Judaism - Bibleism, Prophetism - Newarism, Newarism - Bibleism, Injudaism - New Judaism,** etc. For religions (1) to (11), based on the Ten Commandments, there may be those that interpret the prohibition of adultery as a prohibition of only adultery, and also allow drawing - just do not make an idol out of what is drawn, but starting with **Prophetism** (for some, possibly from New Judaism), the requirements for the Sabbath are also reduced: **Light Newarism, Light Prophetism, Light Biblelism,** etc. Also, those who believe that God judges us and gives us punishment already during this life (for example, in Yom Kippur, as in Judaism), can use the prefix Karma before the name of the religion: **Karma - Bibleism (Bibleism - Karmaism), Karma - Newarism (Newarism - Karmaism),** etc., or they do not believe in the afterlife at all: **New Judaism - Sadducism, Bibleism - Sadducism,** etc. For those who believe in paradise and hell, the word Parahel can be added: **Parahell - New Judaism, Parahell - Prophetism, Parahell - Bibleism,** etc. For those who believe in paradise, albeit through purgatory for sinners, it is simply **Paradise: Paradise - New Judaism, Paradise - Bibleism,** etc. For those who believe in the chain of reincarnations - Samsara: **Samsara - New Judaism, Samsara - Bibleism,** etc. For those who believe in different lengths of soul life for good people and for sinners - Langs: **Langs - New Judaism, Langs - Bibleism,** etc. For those who believe that someday they will be awakened for a new life in paradise, those who deserve it - Wakeup: **Wakeup - New Judaism, Wakeup - Bibleism,** etc. In addition, for most religions, there may be trends that believe that the Ten Commandments are the minimum necessary for fulfillment (perhaps only they are from God, the rest is from man): **Ten-Injudaism, Ten-Prophetism, Ten-Newarism,** etc. For **New Judaism**, this is its version of **Ten (Tentism)**. Likewise, it is **Light-Ten** (Light-Ten, Light-Tenthism): **Light-Ten Injudaism, Light-Ten Prophetism,** etc. For **New Judaism,** it is simply **Lighten** or **Light-Ten.** There may also be directions that believe that God personally administers judgment only in special cases, i.e., that most often the court is ruled by numerous helpers of God (not necessarily the gods themselves, clearly superior to people in their abilities), but he only organizes and controls this process - they can add before the name of the religion, for example, the word Number: **Number - New Judaism, Number - Prophetism, Number - Bibleism.** Speaking personally about me, I consider myself an agnostic, a **Uphist,** very close to **Uarism, Punishism, Karmaism, Prolongism, Langsism, Real Langsism. Punishism - New Judaism, Punishism - New Buddhism, Punishism - Bibleism, Punishism - New Judaism, Punishism - Injudaism, Punishism - Newarism, Punishism - Judaism, Punishism - Prophetism and just Injudaism, New Judaism, General Judaism, Bibleism,** and **Prophetism** are not excluded. Since I do not really believe that God alone, without numerous helpers, can control our entire vast world and see and know everything about everyone, then everything that relates to faith in God - with the prefix Number: **Number - New Judaism, Number - Bibleism, Punishism - Number Injudaism,** etc. As I already wrote, I am really worried about only two questions - **how to live so as not**

to be punished (if punishment exists), and **whether there is an afterlife**, and also whether the punishment is carried out during this life or during the afterlife. The question of how and by what forces this takes place does not really bother me. I absolutely do not believe in the Trinity. **Three persons cannot be a single person at the same time**. And the transformation by God of one of his companions into a sperm or an embryo and its introduction into the body of an earthly woman, although possible, is unlikely.

As you can see, I tried to present all possible options to you. This will probably be rather boring for many of you, and you will simply flip through these pages without reading them carefully. But I am sure that there will be people for whom it will be very important to understand the options presented by me and who will draw important conclusions for themselves. The thought of this spurred my desire to understand the existing religions and present the results to your judgment.

Among the religions presented to you, there are two main approaches. One of them is to strive to unite the maximum number of religions and thereby increase the number of adherents. These are the embracing religions since New Judaism. Another approach is by no means to include in religion those beliefs that might cause mistrust. As you can imagine, I take a mixed approach. It consists in excluding those options that cause the greatest mistrust or categorical rejection, but to combine those that have a chance to correspond to the truth. Based on this approach, it turns out that the most real and, at the same time, sufficiently embracing religions are, for those who believe in God, **New Judaism and Bibleism**, as well as, to a certain extent, Injudaism, Judaism, Newarism, Prophetism, Judaism - Bibleism, Judaism - Newarism and General Judaism, and in general terms - **Uarism (United Religion), Punishism** with its real variants (from Punishism - Injudaism to Punishism - Biblicalism) and **Prolongism**. I think **New Judaism** is the most real religion that has the greatest degree of correspondence to reality, and I am certainly of its first place. But **Bibleism and Newarism** are good for increasing the number of followers and can more realistically provide an alternative to the false directions of Christianity, which consider Jesus to be God Himself. If we talk about the need to unite all or almost all believers, then for this there is a **United Religion, Uarism**, and it's a kind of **Punishism**, uniting those who believe in punishment for sins (all options), as well as the **Prolongism** religion, uniting those who believe in life after death (all options). I still consider myself a Uphist since I oscillate between **Uarism and Agnosticism-Uphism**.

In my opinion, the masses of believers should understand the rationality of what was said and turn to one of the religions I recommend, rejecting what is contrary to common sense or the most convincing of all existing testimonies of God. This would greatly enhance the prestige of religion. The main meaning of religion is a person's understanding of responsibility for their actions. Human souls crave true religion. My task was - to outline the circle of religions that can correspond to the truth. And those who clearly cannot correspond to the truth. Which I did. As can be seen from the table, religions that, in my opinion, can hardly correspond to the truth, are religions from (8) to (21). In principle, from them, for "political" reasons (primarily based on the task of uniting people), one can also exclude the "embracing" religions (groups of religions) Bibliotheism, Bibliocentrism, and Baha'ism (primarily these three), also Unitism, Universalism, Theism, and Influism. But even if all embracing religions are left on the list, **there remains a list of groups of religions that certainly cannot correspond to the truth**. These are Evangelical Christianity, Christianity (Catholicism and Orthodoxy), Non-Biblical Monotheism, Poly-Monotheism, Hinduism, Polytheism and Planetism. To my regret, the overwhelming majority of believers belong to Evangelical Christianity, Christianity (Catholicism and Orthodoxy), Non-Biblical Monotheism (mainly to Islam) and Hinduism.

The same goes for belief in life after death. Belief in life after death can only be based on the belief that the **soul exists**, all other versions must be rejected. I don't want to upset anyone, hurt anyone's religious feelings. You want to believe in what seems right to you, what helps you in life - please believe. I do not impose anything on anyone. But this is my opinion, and I have the right to express it. Unfortunately, the list of "unfounded" religions also includes Evangelical Christianity, dear to my heart, which does not reject the Old Testament and helps Israel survive in a hostile world. But, as they say, the truth is more expensive. It would be very important if even the Evangelical Christians renounced the Trinity. I think this would increase the prestige of the religion and bring new followers to it. However, I believe that each of you can independently figure it out and make the right choice. So, the choice is yours.

In conclusion, I want to repeat once again: A person's moral character and behavior depend on two main factors: on upbringing (family, school, books, television, and other media, etc.) and on religion, the belief that bad behavior will have to answer (the genetic factor probably also takes place, perhaps the astrological one too, but they do not depend on us). From this point of view, any humanistic religion is a blessing, and I welcome all such religions. My denial of a number of religions is only a desire to identify those religions that have a chance to correspond to the truth. It is clear that the greatest chances for this have the unifying religions of **Uarism (United Religion), Prolongism,** and **Uarism - Prolongism**, and for those who believe in God - **New Judaism, Newarism,** and **Bibleism.**